LITERATURE FROM CRESCENT MOON

Sexing Hardy: Thomas Hardy and Feminism
by Margaret Elvy

Thomas Hardy's Jude the Obscure: A Critical Study
by Margaret Elvy

Thomas Hardy's Tess of the d'Urbervilles: A Critical Study
by Margaret Elvy

Stepping Forward: Essays, Lectures and Interviews
by Wolfgang Iser

Lawrence Durrell: Between Love and Death, Between East and West
by Jeremy Mark Robinson

Andrea Dworkin
by Jeremy Mark Robinson

German Romantic Poetry: Goethe, Novalis, Heine, Hölderlin
by Carol Appleby

Feminism and Shakespeare
by B.D. Barnacle

D.H. Lawrence: Infinite Sensual Violence
by M.K. Pace

D.H. Lawrence: Symbolic Landscapes
by Jane Foster

Andre Gide: Fiction and Fervour in the Novels
by Jeremy Mark Robinson

Amorous Life: John Cowper Powys and the Manifestation of Affectivity
by H.W. Fawkner

Postmodern Powys: New Essays on John Cowper Powys
by Joe Boulter

Rethinking Powys: Critical Essays on John Cowper Powys
edited by Jeremy Mark Robinson

Thomas Hardy and John Cowper Powys: Wessex Revisited
by Jeremy Mark Robinson

Julia Kristeva: Art, Love, Melancholy, Philosophy, Semiotics
by Kelly Ives

Luce Irigaray: Lips, Kissing, and the Politics of Sexual Difference
by Kelly Ives

Helene Cixous I Love You: The Jouissance of Writing
by Kelly Ives

Emily Dickinson: Selected Poems
selected and introduced by Miriam Chalk

Dante: *Selections From the Vita Nuova*
translated by Thomas Okey

Friedrich Hölderlin: *Selected Poems*
translated by Michael Hamburger

Rainer Maria Rilke: *Selected Poems*
translated by Michael Hamburger

Samuel Beckett Goes Into the Silence

Samuel Beckett Goes Into the Silence

Jeremy Mark Robinson

Crescent Moon

CRESCENT MOON PUBLISHING
P.O. Box 1312, Maidstone
Kent, ME14 5XU
Great Britain, www.crmoon.com

First published November 5, 1992. Second edition 2020.
© Jeremy Mark Robinson, 1992, 2020.

Set in Bodoni Book 10 on 14pt.
Designed by Radiance Graphics.

The right of Jeremy Mark Robinson to be identified as the author of *Samuel Beckett Goes Into the Silence* has been asserted generally in accordance with sections 77 and 78 of the Copyright, Designs and Patents Act 1988.

All rights reserved. No part of this book may be reprinted or reproduced, stored in a retrieval system, or transmitted, in any form or by any means, electronic, mechanical, photocopying, recording or otherwise, without permission from the publisher.

British Library Cataloguing in Publication data

Robinson, Jeremy
Samuel Beckett Goes Into the Silence
I. Title
828.912

ISBN-13 9781861717771 (Pbk)
ISBN-13 9781861717870 (Hbk)

CONTENTS

Note On Texts ❖ 8
Acknowledgements ❖ 8
Abbreviations ❖ 9
Author's Note ❖ 11

Beginning One ❖ 17
Beginning Two ❖ 20
Beginning Three ❖ 23
Shot One: Language ❖ 26
Shot Two: Philosophy ❖ 87
Ending One ❖ 105
Ending Two ❖ 108

Illustrations ❖ 110
Quotes By Samuel Beckett ❖ 119
Bibliography ❖ 122

NOTE ON TEXTS

English texts of Samuel Beckett's texts have been used. There are many problems considering Beckett's French and English, and the relationships between them are complex.

ACKNOWLEDGEMENTS

To Faber & Faber; Pan Books; John Calder (Publishers); Penguin Books; Macmillan; Allen & Unwin; Oxford University Press' Princeton University Press; and other publishers quoted.

Thanks to Chris Fassnidge and Mandie Robinson.

ABBREVIATIONS

Prose	*Collected Shorter Prose*
Poems	*Collected Poems, 1930-1978*
Works	*The Complete Dramatic Works*
D	*Disjecta: Miscellaneous Writings*
WG	*Waiting For Godot*
Proust	*Proust and Three Dialogues*
Mur	*Murphy*
W	*Watt*
T	*The Beckett Trilogy: Molloy, Malone Dies, The Unnamable*
E	*The Expelled and Other Novellas*
How	*How It Is*
C	*Company*
Ill	*Ill Seen Ill Said*
Who	*Worstward Ho*
MC	*Mercier and Camier*
Story	*As the Story Was Told*
Kicks	*More Pricks Than Kicks*

AUTHOR'S NOTE

This book is an introduction to the art of Samuel Beckett, focussing on: (1) his language and fiction, and (2) the aspects of religion and philosophy in his writing. Examples from throughout Beckett's literary career are included.

This book was originally published in 1992. It has been completely rewritten, and some sections have been updated. I have retained some of the quirky elements (such as the opening and closing passages).

   Jeremy Mark Robinson
   Kent, England

Samuel Beckett

BEGINNING ONE

End it again, you might start like that, start at least like that, or like this, anyway it's a start, I mean, it's a life, of sorts, no one can deny that, but there is no one, no voice, no sound, nothing, and even that's not certain, but this is a start, it's a life, it's a sort of life, can't comment on that, that's a fact, you might start like that, I can't start like that, like this, I can't go on, well go on then, start at least like that, make a start, feel better, make a stain on the silence, a scratch, a cry, some kind of sound, a noise, nothing more, nothing more than that, it's a start, at least it's a start, at least I've started, that is, I mean to say, not I, because this is not me, like all the others, all what others?, all those others, those other voices, well begin again and end it this way, it's a start at least, like this, all those others, well name them then, I could name them, I might, I will, I can't go on, but today I'll go on, I'll name them, all those others, Molloy, Malone, Clov, Mercier, Camier, Krapp, Didi, Belacqua, Watt, Murphy, Mahood, Worm, Pozzo, Lucky, Estragon, Hamm, Nell, Nagg, Mr Rooney, Moran, Godot, the Unnamable… there's so many of them, all those voices, those people, those more-than-people, and why not mention a few other names while you're at it, why not drag 'em all out of the cupboards, Joyce, Woolf, Dante, Lawrence, Stein, Sterne, Conrad, why not have a ball and name them all, there's always more, Proust, van Velde, Wittgenstein, Yeats, Vico, Swift, Kafka, Goethe, Shakespeare, Kant, Heidegger, Nietzsche, Rimbaud, Schopenhauer, Jouve, Flaubert, Stendhal, Baudelaire, Dickens, Diderot, Plato, Aristotle, Bruno, Rilke, Valéry, Éluard, Gide,

Christ it makes me puke to even think of them, all those names, all those voices, all those minds ticking away beyond the grave, beneath the wet grass, six feet under, all dead and buried and gone, of no use to anyone, but even I, I say I, say not I, meaning not me, even I, not I, admit to having a soft spot for one or two of those names, say them again, end it, stop, go, go on, I'll go on, I'll say them, bugger it, it doesn't matter, I'll say the names I like, the names that not-I loves to dream of, I'll say them, I'll do it, it's easy, it's easy to speak, to think, to not think at all, to say the ones I love, I know who they are, Dante, Proust, Joyce, that's the names I like, maybe add a couple more, no more than that, just a couple more, and only from time to time, only when it's too dark to see in here, van Velde and Yeats, but only from time to time, end it again stop defeat I said that, at least it's a start, though I haven't really begun, not really started to really speak, that's a dream, really speaking is a dream of those who wish to stain the silence with a scream, but that's at least a start, at least I've begun, to puke out the not-I voice, to vomit onto the silence, there, that's what works, what works well, even here, in this dark space, I could quote, for what good it'll do, I could quote you from a previous voice, a previous now-dead name:

> I'll say it's I, perhaps it will be I, perhaps that's all they're waiting for, there they are again, to give me quittance, waiting for me to say I'm somewhere, to put me out, into the silence, I see nothing, it's because there is nothing... (T, 378)

BEGINNING TWO

God: I see you've started then.

Dog: Oh, you're awake. Yes, I've started. Like this.

God: Very nice. When will it be finished?

Dog: You make me sick! *(He spits)* 'Finished'? Nothing is ever *finished.* I've only just started, I told you, today, like any other day.

God: The beginning is the best part.

Dog: True.

God: I remember seeing –

Dog: Don't tell me! Now, where did you put our bicycle?

God: We don't have a bicycle.

Dog: We do. You ride on the luggage rack because of your bad leg.

God: Which leg?

Dog: Your right leg. It was always the right leg. It was. But our bicycle is gone. Too bad. I need it for my book.

God: You are writing a book?

Dog: Yes. I told you. I've just started.

God: What is it about?

Dog: You make me sick with your feeble questions! *(He spits. God recoils)* A book, any book, what does it matter what it's about? Death, pain, waiting, loss, illness, anguish. It's all the same, between the womb and the tomb. Do you hear?

God: Am I in it?

Dog: *(Laughs)* Of course you are. Now get up.

God: *(Now standing)* Shall we go?

Dog: Yes, let's go.

God: You first.

Dog: I'll take my book with me.

God: Yes, your play.

Dog: Play? Poem, letter, novel, essay – it doesn't matter now. It's unreadable. I mean, unsayable. I mean, undoable.

God: Who wrote it?

Dog: The Unnamable.

God: I've met him.

Dog: Who? The Unnamable?

God: No, Beckett.

Dog: Oh, this is interminable! This is awful! Let's go. *(Turns to leave)*.

God: Yes, let's go. *(Tries to walk)*. Damn. I can't go.

Dog: I forgot. You can't walk. I'll have to carry you. If only we had our bicycle.

God: Let me sit a while. *(He sits)*.

Dog: *(Picks up a piece of paper and tears it)*. I'll begin again. That was no good. I can't think tonight.

God: Is it night already?

Dog: Yes. Already.

God: This is awful! Nothing happens! Let's go. *(He tries to stand up, and gives up after a moment)*.

Dog: We'll stay here tonight.

God: Yes. *(Yawns)* How will you begin your book?

Dog: I could try quoting –

God: NO! I'll be sick. You know I hate other people's words. Don't read to me, don't quote to me, just stay with me.

Dog: *(Sits beside God)* Yes. I'll stay with you.

God: *(Sleepily)* Shall we go in the morning?

Dog: Yes, we'll go. Sleep now. *(He looks at God)* Good, he's asleep.

BEGINNING THREE

all that falling
all that coming and going
those endless footfalls
close of a long day
everything fading to black
right down
time she stopped
time we began
this is a beginning
at the end of the day
the close of a long day
endless twilight
with nothing between
those are the spaces to live in
we/ he/ she/ you can end now
we've done with waiting
for the dog/ God
mother rocker
done with all that fall
done with that
closed eyes closed
a hole in the ground
all dark no begging
shine on him, eh Joe?

even this is a beginning
time we began
time she stopped
Beckett wants to say
fuck life
so let him say it
end again this way begin

SHOT ONE

LANGUAGE

You might start like that, by pastiching Samuel Beckett (Apl 13, 1906, Dublin - Dec 22, 1989, Paris) in a number of ways. It's a start. There's no denying that. It's a start to a book. Begin by lightly taking off Beckett of the *Unnamable* and the *Texts for Nothing* period. Then try something in the manner of *Waiting For Godot*. Finish up in the style of the later works: *Footfalls* and *Rockaby*.

It's a beginning, at least. Because it's difficult to know where to begin with Mr Samuel Barclay Beckett. He is regarded as pretty much the greatest of modern and postmodern writers, pretty much the world's greatest modern dramatist, and the maybe greatest modern prose stylist. There are many competitors, such as Julia Kristeva, Ursula Le Guin, and Hélène Cixous, but Beckett comes top of many critics' lists.

What more can be said about him? A lot, it seems, judging by the amount of critical works being written about Beckett. It's not all wonderful, of course. Sam Beckett's poetry, for instance, is disappointing, especially when you put it beside Rainer Maria Rilke, Paul Éluard, Robert Graves or Pablo Neruda.

There are few letters by Samuel Beckett in collected books (unlike the many collections of letters by André Gide, say, or Henry Miller). There are few essays (more have been published since Beckett's death in 1989). Instead, we have poems, prose and plays. Or 'works', which is a better (and more Beckettian) name for his productions.

But the most fascinating and the most ironic thing about Samuel Beckett and Samuel Beckett criticism is that most of his art pivots around the dialectic of speaking/ not-speaking, or doing and not-doing, or writing and not-writing. It is ironic that this writer who so desperately wanted to stop writing should create around him such a large amount of writing.

Samuel Beckett is a mass of contradictions. Or at least his art is, not the man. Any Beckett criticism must constantly qualify itself, and contradict itself. This is what Beckett does continually in his art. He says one thing, then states its opposite. Nothing is certain. There are no absolutes. Everything is in flux, in a Heraclitan turmoil.

Why is Samuel Beckett so admired and so significant as a writer? One reason is simple: he's brilliant. Another is his works are very entertaining and very pleasurable to consume. Another is his aims and values in literature were the highest, and deadly serious – he really was aiming to create outstanding art. He is a true writer's writer. Another is his works are very inspiring.

Samuel Beckett's art veers constantly between light and dark. Not between good and evil, but between different states of being. He is not a dualist in the moral sense, but a Hegelian dialectician. He is restless, never satisfied. In the philosophy of the ancient Greek philosopher Empodecles the world moves from Strife to Love and back again. In the Beckettverse there is always Strife, followed by more Strife. Maybe a respite now and then. But not for long. Beckett's is a world of pain. It is also a non-world of no-pain.

From *The Trilogy* (*Molloy-Malone Dies* and *The Unnamable*, 1951-53) onwards, the opposite is also true, as in Jungian psychology. 'But in symbolism, as in life, everything is continuously changing into its opposite,' wrote Tom Chetwynd in *A Dictionary of Symbols* (271). Thus in Beckett's worldview, we find statements and anti-statements, voices and silences, being and non-being, doing and non-doing, light and dark.

Samuel Beckett is the most argumentative, the most anti-anything of writers. His protagonists were there, but were not there. The things happened, yet they did not happen. The book is a fiction, yet it is not a fiction. Typical is the ending of *Molloy* (1951):

> Then I went back into the house and wrote. It is midnight. The rain is beating on the windows. It was not midnight. It was not raining. (T, 162)

It is not a question of was it real/ was it not real? The problem is largely linguistic. So the question is: was it said/ not said? Was it I/ not I? Was it remembered or written, or not remembered or written? From thesis Beckett speeds to antithesis; the synthesis becomes a new thesis, and so on. Instant and eternal opposition. As soon as something is stated, Beckett can't resist stating its opposite. He is always chasing a resolution of the dialectical methodology which will never occur. No closure, no ending, nothing is finished – yet the desire, above all other desires, is to get it all over, to finish it all, to say, like the dying Christ on the Cross, 'It is finished' (*Gospel of St John*, 19:30).

The opening lines of *Endgame* (1957) are: 'Finished, it's finished, nearly finished, it must be nearly finished' (Works, 93). In the play *Footfalls* (1975) the woman's voice asks M(ay):

> V: Will you never have done? (Pause.) Will you never have done... revolving it all?
> M: (Halting.) It?
> V: It all. (Pause.) In your poor mind. (Pause.) It all. (Pause.) It all. (Works, 400)

The 'it' of Samuel Beckett's art is everything, 'it all', the whole thing, life, the going-on, the effort, the endless journey. It's often the same old story in Beckett's writings, the same old things, which come up time and time again. There's no escape, though escape is sometimes yearned for. Instead there is more of the same. And again some more, and then some... more... and again. Even the very short pieces, such as *Ping* or *Still*, are immensely repetitious. But this is part of Beckett's ploy: to get beyond that final synthesis, to move beyond the confines of the dialectic method. To deny unity is to deny an end to ontological restlessness. Beckett never gets *there*, never resolves *it*, never finishes.

Samuel Beckett could have stopped writing, and most of his characters wish to stop writing/ speaking/ creating/ communicating.

But they don't stop speaking. Like their creator, they go on. The final words of Beckett's major prose work, *The Trilogy*, are not 'I can't go on', but: 'I'll go on' (T, 382). So Beckett goes on. Right up until the end.

For Samuel Beckett's protagonists, speaking is the same as living. One cannot live without speaking; one cannot speak without being alive. The paradoxes multiply. For Beckett himself writing might have been synonymous with living. He was not an obsessive journal writer, like Anaïs Nin or André Gide, but he did write throughout most of his life. He did not, like Jean Sibelius or Friedrich Hölderlin or Carl-Theodore Dreyer, stop creating for years. Like his characters, he went on – and on.

Writers such as Anaïs Nin and André Gide wrote continuously – their *Journals* are gigantic works. If Sam Beckett is not like that, his characters are. They talk and talk and talk. Even though many of them yearn for silence above anything else, they still talk. Or write. Or babble inside their skulls. *The Trilogy* in particular is full of voices that never stop speaking.

In Samuel Beckett's world, René Descartes' famous dictum is changed to: 'I speak, therefore I am'. Being is speaking, saying is inventing, talking is living. Beckett's people don't have problems with action, with doing. They don't feel guilty about not 'doing' anything. They 'do' very little.

To speak or keep silent, to move or to stay still – these are some of the decisions facing Samuel Beckett's protagonists. They are simple problems which create complex metaphysical thoughts and dilemmas. Part of the fascination of Beckett's output is his ability to work on so many levels at the same time. While he concentrates on compressing all he wants to say into a small space, everything else – the discourses, philosophies, issues and speculations – expand ever more rapidly. With Beckett's work, less certainly is more. His art is full of scenes in which 'nothing happens' and yet he is exalted as a great artist.

More irony: Samuel Beckett's three literary heroes, Marcel Proust and James Joyce and Dante Alighieri, wrote and over-wrote *Bible*-sized works. *Ulysses*, *Remembrance of Things Past* and *The Divine Comedy* are long and large artworks which aim to be comprehensive, to include everything in the world and in life. Only Beckett's *Trilogy* approaches the length of the major works of Proust, Joyce or Dante, but much of Beckett's art aims to be just as comprehensive and all-inclusive. His short works, such as *Lessness* or *Imagination Dead Imagine*, seem very long because of their depth. (Beckett is a 'vertical' author – depth not width. Not ranging over a wide area, but going deeper into the same space again and again).

Samuel Beckett doesn't aim for that comprehensive verisimilitude of James Joyce or Marcel Proust, in which the world of childhood and early adulthood is so lovingly and richly evoked, but he does go for a detailed, compressed, rich image. The sense of life being lived is still there, but pictured in a different way.

The link between writing and living is deeper and more complex in Samuel Beckett's art than in most writers's work. André Gide's *The Counterfeiters* (1925) features a novelist who makes copious notes on his novel: the record of the making of the book will be more interesting than the book itself, he claims (*The Counterfeiters*, 170). For Gide's novelist, life is not real or meaningful unless it has been noted down (ib., 142).

Much of Samuel Beckett's art features recording processes: film, video, audio tape, digital recording, and writing. Vladimir says in *Waiting For Godot*: 'At me too someone is looking' (WG, 91). Tape playback features in dramas such as *Eh, Joe, Rockaby* and *Krapp's Last Tape*.

The observer, the gaze, the listener, and the ear are essential in the artistic world of Samuel Beckett. As in the cinema of Alfred Hitchcock, Dario Argento or Walerian Borowczyk and in the fiction of Thomas Hardy, there is always someone looking or listening in Samuel Beckett's œuvre. The audience is always there, somewhere in the text. Beckett always writes with an ear and eye in mind. Even in the claustrophic spaces of texts such as *All Strange Away* or *Ping*, there is an audience.

Some people complain that Samuel Beckett gives his audience a hard time. Not so, he always involves his audience deeply. He might berate his audience sometimes or use the distancing or alienation devices of the theatre of Bertholt Brecht and Antonin Artaud, but he doesn't negate them completely. In texts such as *The Unnamable* and

Cascando, we are taken into intimate contact with the narrator/s and voice/s.

The enmeshment of reader, text, character and author is deep in Samuel Beckett's art. Because there is always someone looking at us, and behind them, someone else is looking at them. It is like a hall of mirrors, self-reflexivity taken to extremes.

Samuel Beckett's prose style is intriguing. He pushes language to its limits, like Gertrude Stein, James Joyce, Paul Valéry and William Burroughs. Beckett develops the philosophies of language propounded by Ludwig Wittgenstein, Karl Kraus and Stéphane Mallarmé. Part of Beckett's enduring fascination for cultural theorists, semioticians, post-structuralists and other postmodern critics, is due to his unending exploration of language, language systems, intertextuality, meaning and re/presentation. Beckett stalks through a world of words whirling between Jacques Lacan's and Julia Kristeva's symbolic and imaginary realms. Like an autist stuck in the Lacanian mirror phase, Beckett wades through a swamp of Barthesian signifieds and codes. (Certainly, the entry into the symbolic realm, *pace* Julia Kristeva's philosophy, is one of the chief journeys – and struggles – of Beckett's art. The urge to speak, to share something, to make a connection cannot be ignored if the subject wishes to remain human. Socialization is mandatory, and Beckett's art pivots around such tensions, between speaking and not speaking, between being and doing, between solitude and society).

Samuel Beckett takes up the tenets of the Symbolist writers of the *fin-de-siècle* (musicality, economy, rhythm), such as Paul Valéry, Guillaume Apollinaire and Stéphane Mallarmé, moves through the modernist, self-conscoius improvizations of James Joyce and T.S. Eliot, and goes beyond them into post-WW2 abstraction. As Jacques Lacan said in *Écrits*, in a Nietzschean mode, 'the world of words... creates the world of things' (65). This is true in Beckett's case, where, often, there is no other world beyond the world of words. Few authors are so wrapped up in the syntactics, the structure and form of words and word-systems. However, as we shall see, Beckett is also a storyteller, and even in his most abstract pieces (such as *How It Is, Ping* and *Lessness*), he is still telling some kind of a story.

Samuel Beckett's writing style has some of the lucidity of Stendhal and Gustave Flaubert; the musicality of Paul Verlaine and Stéphane Mallarmé; the vivacity and invention of James Joyce and Henry Miller; the anger and societal rebellion of Charles Baudelaire and William Burroughs; and the hypnotism of Virginia Woolf and D.H. Lawrence.

Samuel Beckett has affinities with the stream of consciousness method of Virginia Woolf, John Cowper Powys, D.H. Lawrence and James Joyce. The hypnotic repetition and musicality, the compressed lucidity and wild idiosyncracies of these writers are found in the writings of Beckett. In Woolf's short story *The Fascination of the Pool*, we find an image out of Beckett's art – a voice being heard in a pool. But it is told in a simple, uncluttered style, with a minimum of punctuation, as in Beckett's work:

> So sad a voice must come from the very bottom of the pool. It raised itself under the others as a spoon lifts all the things in a bowl of water. This was the voice we all wished to listen to. (227)

The imagery – of the past, voices, water, and a strange kind of communication – has equivalents in the work of Samuel Beckett, although the latter would not use a phrase such as 'so sad', which drips of too-easy sentiment. At times, though, Beckett assumes the quiet stridency of Virginia Woolf's tone.

But how about comparing Samuel Beckett and D.H. Lawrence? It seems ridiculous. Nothing could be further from Beckett's super-minimal, super-restrained, super-compressed art than Lawrence's effusive, over-the-top, over-written, erotic, polemical, and prophetic (preachy) visions. There's nothing in Beckett's *œuvre* that comes close to a sentence (from *The Rainbow*) such as: 'She was very beautiful then, so wide opened, so radiant, so palpitating, exquisitely vulnerable and poignantly, wrongly, throwing herself at risk' (348). Go Lawrence!

That sort of emotion would make Samuel Beckett-the-artist vomit. To such an austere, held-in writer, such over-blown passions are obscene. Yet Beckett too uses such repetitions – the constant incantation of beloved words, which's one of the primary ingredients of Bertie Lawence's prose style (Lawrence repeats words in a different order to reach what he's aiming for; Beckett also uses a lot of repetition). While Lawrence uses a vocabulary packed full of terms such as *passion, wildness, touch, blood* and *desire*, Beckett prefers *nothing, no, grey, black, dead,* and *silence*. Lawrence is a Fauvist or Expressionist painting, all vivid colours and heightened emotions; Beckett is an austere sculpture by Alberto Giacometti (as critics have noted), and later, a Minimal painting by North American artists such as Robert Ryman or Ad Reinhardt.

Like D.H. Lawrence (and like John Cowper Powys, Emily Brontë and J.G. Ballard), Samuel Beckett evokes the elemental powers of nature – the wind, rain, clouds and skies. Lawrence's and Beckett's characters have a restlessness and ontological dissatisfaction in common. 'Paul was dissatisfied with himself and with everything', Lawrence wrote in *Sons and Lovers* (271). This is the starting point of most of Beckett's art (and much of modern literature). Vladimir, Hamm, Winnie, Molloy, the Unnamable – they are eternally dissatisfied people (satisfaction simply does not exist in Beckett's fictive world).

Although Samuel Beckett is ideologically, socially and psychologically a very different writer from D.H. Lawrence, he did produce pieces of intense lyricism. Late works such as *Ill Seen, Ill Said* and *Stirrings Still*, are as lyrical as the poesie of Francesco Petrarch or Johann Wolfgang von Goethe. The piece *Stirrings Still* (1988) ends:

> You go back into your mind. So too did you but know it has closed her eyes. So you sit face to face in the little summerhouse. With eyes closed and hands on knees. In the bloom of your adulthood. In that rainbow light. That dead still. (Prose, 206-7)

Typical of Samuel Beckett to add 'that dead still' at the end. D.H. Lawrence and sunnier authors might have left it at 'rainbow light'. But as Beckett's piece shifts between the present and the past, he naturally finishes in the present, on a note of unmelodramatic melancholy. Because that's how it is.

Sometimes Samuel Beckett's prose, in its rigidity and unfussy flow, resembles the sturdy style of Thomas Hardy. At its best, Hardy's style is dry, matter-of-fact, ironic. Like Beckett's, it aims at presentation, not representation. As in *Tess of the d'Urbervilles*

> Several days had passed since her futile journey, and Tess was afield. The dry winter wind still blew, but a screen of thatched hurdles erected in the eye of the blast kept its force away from her. (392)

Like Samuel Beckett, Thomas Hardy spends a good deal of time describing spaces in detail. Both writers image up solitary travellers on open roads; both writers have links with Gnosticism and philosophers such as Arthur Schopenhauer; both are atheists; both kick against the pricks of Christianity, the establishment and intolerance; both have a sophisticated metaphysics of light and dark; both continually invoke the observer and the observed; both are highly visual writers; both invoke painting; both are regarded as pessimists (whereas they are realists), and so on.

Although Thomas Hardy didn't write 'fuck life' as Samuel Beckett did, it is certainly part of the message of polemical late novels such as *Tess of the d'Urbervilles* and *Jude the Obscure*. Tess tells her younger brother on the cart that we live on a blighted planet (70). Beckett would agree with that. The hanging of Jude's children (a truly grotesque scene) in *Jude the Obscure* finds a parallel in *Waiting For Godot* (WG, 17, 93).

But the deepest connection between the worlds of Thomas Hardy and Samuel Beckett is their bizarre (post-)Gnostic belief in being *unborn*. How many times, in the works of Hardy and Beckett, have we heard characters moaning that they wished they'd never been born? It's a notion of hopelessness not found in such a passionate degree in almost any other major writers.

While one aspect of Samuel Beckett's style is musical compression, as found in the poetry of Guillaume Apollinaire and Paul Valéry, there is also a tendency to over-the-top over-writing, as in the prose of James Joyce, John Cowper Powys and Henry Miller. Beckett likes to write in a bombastic, arrogant tone occasionally. In his novel *Sexus*, book one of *The Rosy Crucifixion* trilogy, Miller conjures many verbal conceits which Beckett might enjoy (and indeed probably did):

> She stoops to stroke the head of a dove, so soft and feathery, so warm with

love, a piece of blood wrapped in velvet... They hissed their long polychromatic words through tiny, sensual mouths whose lips were soft as geraniums... The sun was setting in the West as usual, not in splendour and radiance however but in disgust, like a gorgeous omelet engulfed by clouds of snot and phlegm... I took off my shoes and leisurely deposited my big toe in the first notch of Mara's crotch. Her head was pointed South, mine North; we pillowed them on folded hands, our bodies relaxed and floating effortlessly in the magnetic drift, like two enormous twigs suspended on the surface of a gasoline lake. (*Sexus*, 84, 87, 144)

Go to, Henry! This is orgiastic/ orgasmic writing, writing as Romantic rebellion which aims to explode the world. Self-consciously arrogant and fey and OTT.

Samuel Beckett created the occasional verbal explosion. Take the apocalyptical ending of *How It Is*, for instance:

no more no answer the silence no answer die no answer DIE screams I MAY DIE screams I SHALL DIE screams good (How, 160).

The orgasmic scream of love/ death, love-and-death, love<—>death in this kind of post-Sadeian, Existential, oh-so cleverly nihilistic writing finds its apotheosis in the fictions of William Burroughs. The American Beat author is the king of apocalyptic, sex-and-death prose fashioned from Pop Art cut-ups and ultra self-conscious, Frenchified avant-gardism. This typical passage from Burroughs' most famous piece, *The Naked Lunch*, shows the influence not only of the Miller and Beckett School, but also of Gertrude Stein:

Mrs. Vandergbligh swatting at a Xiucutil: "Oh! ...Oh!... OOOOOOO-OOOOH!" Screams of breaking glass, ripping cloth. A rising crescendo of grunts and squeals and moans and whimpers and gasps... Reek of semen and cunts and sweat and the musty odour of penetrated rectums... Diamonds and fur pieces, evening dresses, orchids, suits and underwear litter the floor covered by a writhing, frenzied, heaving mass of naked bodies. (170)

•

There are many games in Samuel Beckett's writing: wordplay, punning, jokes, puzzles, plays on the letter 'm' (and 'a'), lists, mathematics, numerical permutations, abstractions, etc. There is a feeling for the shape of sentences, the pattern of paragraphs, and the look of the text on the page. Beckett develops the emphasis on the concrete or visual so important in the poesie of Ezra Pound, Gertrude Stein and T.S. Eliot. Each Beckett text has a particular look: many feature very long paragraphs (*The End* and *Malone Dies*); many are one block of text only (*One Evening* and *He Is Barehead*); plays such as *...but the clouds...* and *Come and Go* feature diagrams and precise instructions on space, layout and design.

While shape and pattern are crucial in the work of Samuel Beckett, he did not sacrifice sense to form. He did not produce concrete or typographic poetry. In his art there is always sense/ meaning/ depth. He was concerned with the structure of words, of sentences, of texts. André Gide spoke of the need to perfect the sentence (*Journal*, 182), while Gertrude Stein made a study of such things.

One senses a resentment for Gertrude Stein amongst those who exalt the Joyce-Beckett School. Maybe partly because Stein was doing what they did years before them (and she was very, very good). She was experimenting with the syntactics, musicality and concretism of words years before Joyce. The resentment perhaps stems from Stein being an American (but this doesn't/ didn't stop people applauding T.S. Eliot) and a woman. There is probably some truth in this. The innovations of Jane Austen and Emily Brontë rely on male writers; similarly, Virginia Woolf comes after James Joyce, in the lit'ry canon. But placing a woman *before* Joyce, no, that is too much. It is not allowed. So Stein is ranked way below. Yet she created some marvellous poetry. This is from her 'Lifting Belly':

> Kiss my lips. She did.
> Kiss my lips again she did.
> Kiss my lips over and over and over again she did.
> I have feathers.
> Gentle fishes.
> Do you think about apricots. We find them very beautiful. It is not alone their color it is their seeds that charm us. We find it a change.
> Lifting belly is so strange.
> I came to speak about it.

And Gertrude Stein said many excellent things about poetry and language:

> Periods have a life of their own a necessity of their own a feeling of their own a time of their own... I have told you that I recognize verbs and adverbs aided by prepositions and conjunctions with pronouns as possessing the whole of the active life of writing. (*Look at me now and here I am*, 128-9)

Gertrude Stein hated question marks, exclamation marks, quotation marks, and, in particular, commas. Much of Samuel Beckett's prose hinges on commas in its structure (*The Unnamable*, for example). In the later short pieces, Beckett does away with commas. Stein's idea was that the sense should be clear enough without the need for excessive punctuation. But Beckett's prose is a poetry of the voice, and relates to speech/ is often speech/ must be spoken aloud/ or spoken internally. The comma, some were taught at school, is a pause for breathing; in Beckett's theatrics, it functions as that – a pause for breath in the incessant flood of spoken words. (As a theatrical director, Beckett would talk about the exact length of pauses, and get into half-pauses, and quarter pauses).

There are other ways in which the poetries of Ms Stein and Mr Beckett chime. 'Nothing makes any difference as long as someone is listening while they are talking', wrote Stein in *Look at me now and here I am* (101), and this applies to Beckett's art.

Stein again:

> Poetry is concerned with using with abusing, with losing with wanting, with denying with avoiding with adoring with replacing the noun. It is doing that always doing that doing that and doing nothing but that. Poetry is doing nothing but using losing refusing and pleasing and betraying and caressing nouns. (ib., 136)

Yes and in the poetics of Samuel Beckett there is one noun/ pronoun that is always being chased/ interrogated/ abused/ yearned for/ re-hashed: 'I'. The 'I, say I' of *The Unnamable* (267), and the 'not I' of the play *Not I* (1972). In this book, I come back again and again to the problem of the 'I'/ ego/ self. But the form of the book is part of the investigation. (What we're really talking is the ultimate character in a Beckett text: the narrator, a character that Philip Pullman calls the most wonderful in literature, superior to any other chara).

The Unnamable is a book that moves towards the state of being a single sentence. Towards the end it gets like that: non-stop words, a million clauses/ sub-clauses/ subordinate clauses, and a hermeneutic restlessness. To quote from the last section of *The Unnamable* is to lose much of the effect (it's too long to quote in full): it is best read it all at once.

Certainly much of the enjoyment of reading the works of Mr Beckett is because he is a master of the sentence, as this example from *The Unnamable* demonstrates:

> Organs, without, it's easy to imagine, a god, it's unavoidable, you imagine them, it's easy, the worst dulled, you doze away, an instant. (T, 280)

Short, sharp phrases here, the choice of words is spot-on, the pacing precise, the result is clear: it is the age-old, Beckettian problem of thesis/ antithesis, deification/ atheism, instant/ eternity, imagination/ death. Eternal, never-to-be-reconciled opposites or opposing ideas/ thoughts/ feelings/ experiences/ things.

In the later works of S.B., the sentences become even more ruthlessly pared down – to the bare bones of language. Each word is forced to carry maximum meaning and yet the sentences teeter on the brink of meaninglessness. The opening of *Imagination Dead Imagine* is especially powerful, with its ragged/ rhythmic punctuation and linguistic precision:

> No trace anywhere of life, you say, pah, no difficulty there, imagination not dead yet, yes, dead, good, imagination dead imagine. Islands, waters, azure, verdure, one glimpse and vanished, endlessly, omit. (Prose, 145)

This is superb, one of my favourite Beckett snippets, as memorable as the best of William Shakespeare, and as memorable as the poesie of Dante Alighieri. Prose-poetry is insufficient a name for it, as it is for Arthur Rimbaud's *Illuminations*. It is best savoured line by line, phrase by phrase, like the poetry of Emily Dickinson or Anna Akhmatova. We could print the opening of *Imagination Dead Imagine* thus, to bring out the language and poise:

> No trace anywhere of life
> you say
> pah
> no difficulty there
> imagination not dead yet
> yes
> dead
> good
> imagination dead imagine.
>
> Islands
> waters
> azure
> verdure
> one glimpse and vanished
> endlessly
> omit.

The shock is suddenly coming across the word 'azure', so rich a word, so rare in Samuel Beckett's vocabulary, with connotations of the troubadour poets, and the blue and gold of Renaissance painting and French royalty. (The quote also reminds us of the significance of writing in French for Beckett, where musicality and sound are key ingredients of poetic effects).

One of the pleasures of Samuel Beckett's texts is this sudden richness. He sets up a vortex of words, words whirling in musical repetitions, then he throws in something really unexpected. Often the unexpected is sexual, or a swear word. 'Fuck life' occurs at the end of *Rockaby* (1981); just as typical is this from *Molloy*:

> When I seek refuge there, beat to the world, all shame drunk, my prick in my rectum, who knows. Good. (T, 20)

This sudden intrusion of sex/ the body/ humour helps the writer to kick her/ his material into life – to add some 'jizz', as Samuel Beckett might say.

After *The Unnamable*, the fiction of Samuel Beckett becomes more and more compressed, reduced, pared-down. There is more and more of less and less. It is impossible to extricate form from content. But then it was always like this with Beckett's work, and with art. In Beckett's *œuvre* the medium is not so much the message as the *presence* Like the sculptures that Tony Smith or Donald Judd made in North America in the 1960s, Beckett's texts are simply *there.* No analysis, no interpretation, no discussion, no 'meaning', no symbols: the sculptures are just *there* (a Judd sculpture is an object, just a thing, with no reference to anything outside of itself). Beckett's words *exist,* they have *presence* As the presentation is reduced, so too are the spaces within the texts: those white walls; tiny boxes/ rotundas/ vaults; bodies cruelly naked; light is all-white or all-black. The vocabulary, which was ostentatiously large in the early works, is reduced drastically. A set of words are repeated. The permutations veer from mathematics to poetry.

Ping and *Lessness* are perhaps the most severely reductive of Samuel Beckett's later texts. A computer could give us an analysis of the number of times words occur, statistical analysis, a line by line breakdown of the structure. Many times Beckett invites such an approach, with his (sometimes tiresome) mathematical games. *For To End Yet Again, Ping, Lessness, Closed Space*- these pieces eject the comma, and concentrate on the unadorned sentence:

light heat hands hanging palms front white on white invisible

...is a typical sentence from *Ping* (1966, Prose, 149). Compare it with one from *For To End Yet Again* (1976)*:*

Grey cloudless sky grey sand as far as eye can see long desert to begin (ib., 179)

Clearly Samuel Beckett is hacking away at the same thing time and time again: an enclosed space, colourless, claustrophobic, static, with one or two people/ bodies/ skulls situated within these spaces, uncommunicating.

The grey-on-grey landscapes of *Lessness*(1970) and *For To End Yet Again* recall the grey marshlands of André Gide's early book *Paludes* (1895). Early on, Gide's writer, struggling to write the book-within-a-book, moans, 'Nothing ever happens!' (30), anticipating *Waiting For Godot* by sixty years. 'The boredom, the emptiness, the monotony' of Gide's book (20), find equivalents in Beckett's grey environments.

The dictum of André Gide's anti-hero, and the dictum of all Gide's protagonists, and most of Samuel Beckett's too, is: 'Once we take up an idea, we must carry it to the very end' (ib., 86). It's pure Romanticism, going to extremes. Beckett did this in *The Trilogy:* each book is more extreme than the last; he went further with *Texts For Nothing*; then *How It Is*, then the very extreme pieces, such as *All Strange Away* and *The Lost Ones*.

Samuel Beckett's most difficult piece is probably *How It Is* (1961), because of its length (160 pages). Its only punctuation is the gaps between each block/ paragraph of text. If it was printed without the gaps it would be nearly unreadable. Even Beckett's short texts require deep concentration (they demand a lot more from the reader than an ad for a Dodge truck or Yahoo's home page).

•

But Samuel Beckett's repetition can be highly poetic. Take *Lessness* for example: the vocabulary is limited to words such as *body, grey, light, ruins, refuge* and *air*. Phrases are repeated, or go through slightly varied permutations:

> Grey face two pale blue little body heart beating only upright... Little body grey face features crack and little holes two pale blue... Little body ash grey locked rigid heart beating face to endlessness... (Prose, 153)

The 'little body' is repeated some 21 times. The heart's beating; the eyes are alive; it's out in the open: although Samuel Beckett maintains this work is about the collapse of a refuge (on the cover of the 1970 edition of the book), it is more optimistic than the claustrophobias of *Ping* and *All Strange Away*.

This emphasis on repetition with slight variations has equivalents in serial and Minimal music (Steve Reich, Phillip Glass, Arvo Pärt, etc); in the seriality of American painters such as Frank Stella, Robert Ryman, Ellsworth Kelly and Brice Marden; in the *avant garde*, experimental cinema of Michael Snow and Andy Warhol; and in the environmental objects of Carl Andre, Donald Judd and Robert Morris.

Still allows itself a larger vocabulary than some of the late works. Despite its matter-of-fact, empirical tone, in which the situation is flatly described, it is a poetic work with many moments of lyricism. The situation, of someone in a chair, is familiar (from *Murphy* to *Endgame* and *Rockaby*). It is a clichéd situation – someone watching a sunset, a set-up which perhaps no one could do anything new with; yet Beckett does.

We have seen many instances where Samuel Beckett takes a cliché and turns it into something fresh. The first line of *Lessness* for example:

Ruins true refuge long last towards which so many false time out of mind. (Prose, 153)

The cliché 'time out of mind' takes on a new meaning in its new context. Perhaps the fascination is that no one before has put those familiar words in that particular order. Perhaps Samuel Beckett tries out all these permutations in order to cover all the ground, all the possibilities. However, he didn't go as far in this anal encyclopædical tendency as James Joyce, who threw masses of trivia into *Ulysses*.

In *Still*, Samuel Beckett creates his most gorgeous sense of surface. There is a beautiful sheen to the text, like the surface of a calm lake or an oil painting by Leonardo da Vinci. Beckett captures the glow in the sky in prose as effectively as painters such as J.M.W. Turner and Emil Nolde do in their watercolour paintings. The imagery is of a sunset and a person watching it, but Beckett is restrained: there are no colours here, only light and dark (the falling and rising of light is of far more metaphysical significance than the colour of the light). Beckett plays with words such as *still till light like bright quite quiet right* (such as in the phrase 'failing light quite still till quite dark', which describes the mood of the piece).

Again, it is still but not static, dark but not utterly black, near dead, not simply dead. As with *Lessness* there a positive stance being evoked here, in this listening/ watching presence:

Bright at last close of a dark day the sun shines out at last and goes down.

> Sitting quite still at valley window normally turn head now and see it the sun low in the southwest sinking. Even get up certain moods and go stand by western window quite still watching it sink and then the afterglow. (Prose, 183)

Once or twice in his rare non-fiction/ non-drama appearances in print, Samuel Beckett explained his creative credo. Probably the best statements on his own art feature in *Three Dialogues* (with Géorges Dutuit):

> The expression that there is nothing to express, nothing with which to express, nothing from which to express, no power to express, no desire to express, together with the obligation to express. (D, 139)

This is Samuel Beckett's artistic conflict elegantly summarized: a series of artistic negatives, followed by an injunction: the obligation to express. Notice he says 'express', not 'communicate'. Although the Beckett protagonist cannot keep silent, despite desiring to do so, s/he also desires communication and relationship. Beckett's battered souls are not simply howling in a vacuum, they are also communicating. Though Beckett says 'express', he also means communicate. Every text creates an audience/ implies an audience/ speaks to an audience. Beckett is very much concerned with his audience. He was very precise about his theatrical drama, for example, demanding that it be performed exactly as written (and in the theatre, the writer is king, with the name over the play's title sometimes, and ahead sometimes of the director and the actors – no way could Beckett have flourished in contemporary Hollywood, for instance – ! – where writers are regularly rewritten and replaced, hired and fired. Imagine Beckett being told by some big-shot film producer than they're going to scrap what he's written and do a page one rewrite with two 24 year-old authors fresh out of U.C.L.A.!).

Another extract from the *Three Dialogues* propounds the dichotomy of nothing to express/ obligation to express in a different manner:

> B. – The situation is that of him who is helpless, cannot act, in the event cannot paint, since he is obliged to paint. The act is of him who, helpless, unable to act, acts, in the event paints, since he is obliged to paint.
> D. – Why is he obliged to paint?

B. – I don't know.
D. – Why is he helpless to paint?
B. – Because there is nothing to paint and nothing to paint with. (D, 142)

This text – a carefully controlled intellectual dialogue – posits the artist as anguished Existentialist, tied down by his/ her own ontological frustration, unable to act yet desiring so much to act, a maker agonized by so many Existential provisos, injunctions and limitations. The end result is a glorification of failure. Samuel Beckett's tenets can never be fulfilled. There must always be agony and failure. Beckett expounds his philosophy of failure thus:

> to be an artist is to fail, as no other dare fail, that failure is his world and the shrink from it desertion, art and craft, good housekeeping, living... I know that all that is required now... is to make of this submission, this admission, this fidelity to failure, a new occasion, a new term of relation, and of the act which, unable to act, obliged to act, he makes, an expressive act, even if only of itself, of its impossibility... (D, 145)

Making art thus becomes not a Romantic rebellion against life, but a post-Einsteinian acquiescence to life, a submission to one's ontology of failure and frustration. Samuel Beckett dives into failure, relishing in failure. His works languish in failure, and his protagonists are cosmic failures.

The manifestation of Samuel Beckett's philosophy of failure is to take literature to its extreme, to go on and on *ad infinitum*, to never never, never stop. Beckett's later art is a series of reductions: of sound, sense, space, style, discourse, and ontology. Style gets sparer; sound becomes brittle, clipped, more abstract; spaces become more and more enclosed; sense narrows; discourse is not allowed to meander – it is firmly attached to a single line of enquiry; ontology moves from death to nothing, from speech to silence. Dip into Beckett's post-*Trilogy* work and you'll probably find something on the eternal speech/ silence conflict. 'You will be quite alone with your voice, there will be no other voice in the world but yours', Ada tells Henry in the play *Embers* (Works, 262), but she continues to speak, unabated. The voice in *Cascando* hovers between speaking and finishing with speaking:

...sleep...no more stories...no more words (ib., 297)

The conflict of speech-versus-silence is at the heart of Samuel Beckett's work. It leads into all the other dialectical and metaphysical problems of being/ doing, action/ non-action, yes/ no, life/ death, now/ then, solitude/ company, desire/ non-desire, etc. Constant striving is the ontological state of Beckett's tortured souls. Always becoming, never resting in pure being. As the philosopher Søren Kierkegaard put it in *Postscripts* 'he strives infinitely, is constantly in process of becoming' (84). Kierkegaard also said: 'during the first period of a man's life the greatest danger is not to take the risk'. As in Existentialism, the concept of being lies at the centre of mysticism. In Beckett's art, being is bound up with language, with speaking. To speak is to be, or to be obliged to speak is to be. Being/ living in Beckett means being obliged to speak.

The emphasis on failure, suffering and speech-and-silence makes Samuel Beckett a religious writer with a bleak, tragic view of life. This is not so much a Christian as a post-Nietzschean view – of the human condition as an essentially tragic one. Friedrich Nietzsche wrote that

> existence is considered sacred enough to justify even a tremendous amount of suffering. (*The Portable Nietzsche,* 459)

Samuel Beckett will not succumb to tragedy so easily, though. His innate sense of the dialectic means he veers from comedy to tragedy easily. The tragic view, he might insist (like the Existentialist philosophers), is merely an honest, realistic one. Beckett is always a realist, even in his most fantastical works. More than a realist, he is a reductionist, though he retains more humanism than, say, Sigmund Freud (one of the modernism's arch reductionists).

Beckett's realism has equivalents in the relativity physics of Albert Einstein. Student engineers have paraphrased the Laws of Thermodynamics thus:

> (1) You can't win, (2) You can't even break even, (3) Things are going to get worse before they get any better, and (4) who says things are going to get better? (J.C Greenstein, 46)

This is Samuel Beckett's philosophical view: things will get worse; it's highly unlikely they'll get any better; in the meantime, let's moan about it – moan because we can't keep quiet.

There are other scientific correspondences with Samuel Beckett: quantum theory, the New Physics, Werner Heisenberg's Uncertainty/ Indeterminacy Principle, Chaos/ Entropy Theory and stochastic process. Beckett spoke about 'the mess', and spoke of art and chaos: 'to find a form that accommodates the mess, that is the task of the artist now' (quoted in L. Graver, *Heritage*, 219).

In Dublin in 1946, Samuel Beckett had a vision of chaos which was a revelation of the nature of his art and its future. He put the experience into his play *Krapp's Last Tape*. An early version of it reads that it was

> clear to me at last that the dark I have been fighting off all this time is in reality my most... unshatterable association till my dying day of story and night with the light of understanding. (in D. Bair, 351)

In the published version the emphasis is slightly different:

> clear to me at last that the dark I have always struggled to keep under is in reality my most – (KRAPP curses, switches off, winds tape forward, switches on again) – unshatterable association until my dissolution of storm and night with the light of understanding and the fire. (Works, 220)

The darkness is realized and embraced. The exploration is of that area between storm/ story/ dark/ light/ noise/ silence.

In traditional, historical mysticism there are three forms of silence: of the mouth, the mind, and the will, as John Ferguson explained in *An Illustrated Encyclopædia of Mysticism* (171). Samuel Beckett's people break all these forms of silence. Like God, they speak the Word, the Creative Word which becomes flesh. Mystics such as Miguel de Molinos (1628-97) and Madame Guyon (1648-1717) were Quietists. The Quietist movement quoted another mystic, Francois de Sales (1567-1622): 'desire nothing, refuse nothing'.

The negation of desire features prominently in Buddhism, a religion which has many correspondences with Sam Beckett's art. His characters desire to stop speaking/ stop living, but despite that they carry on. Desirelessness, the *nirvana* of Oriental mysticism, is never attained in Beckett's art. His charas never quite get beyond the dialectic of opposites; unity is not reached; the urge towards dissolution and chaos never quite negated.

To never end, never finish /stop/ complete/ leave whatever was started, this is the agony of Samuel Beckett the artist. Begin again: the silence is never attained: it remains a dream-silence: the silence that got away: the silence that dangles in front of the eyes like a carrot:

Vladimir: How's the carrot?
Estragon: It's a carrot. (*Waiting For Godot*, 20)

The silence must be virtual/ imaginary/ made by humans; the silence is a dreamland invented by those who cannot stop speaking; the silence is nowhere but you've got to find it; the impossibility of the whole enterprise is beautiful and resembles the Christian theologian Tertullian's precept: 'I believe because it is absurd'. (You might paraphrase Tertullian in Beckettian terms: 'I write because it is absurd', or: 'I am because it is absurd').

The problem has an ethical beauty about it that would naturally fascinate an austere artist. Listen to the way that Samuel Beckett tackles it at the end of his longest and most sustained assault on the unassailable fortress of silence, 1953's *The Unnamable*:

> ...but unconditionally, I resume, so long as, so long as, let me see, so long as one, so long as he, ah fuck all that, so long as this, than that, agreed, that's good enough... it's because you're tired, you want to stop, travel no more, seek no more, lie no more, speak no more, close your eyes... I can't speak of anything, and yet I speak... if it's possible you can do nothing when you want nothing, who cannot hear, cannot speak, who is I, who cannot be I, of whom I can't speak, of whom I must speak, that's all hypotheses, I said nothing, someone said nothing... The silence, a word on the silence, in the silence, that's the worst, to speak of silence... the silence, speak of the silence before going into it, was I there already, I don't know... in the end, it's the end, the ending end, it's the silence, a few gurgles on the silence, the real silence... I won't be the last, I'll be with the others, I'll be as gone, in the silence, it won't be I, it's not I, I'm not there yet, I'll go there now... these are words, open on the silence, straight out, why not, all this time on the brink of silence... Waiting for me to say I'm someone, to say I'm

somewhere, to put me out, into the silence, I see nothing, it's because there is nothing... it will be I, it will be the place, the silence, the end, the beginning, the beginning again, how can I say it, that's all words, they're all I have, and not many of them, the words fail, the voice fails, so be it, I know that well, it will be the silence, full of murmurs, distant cries, the usual silence... or dream, dream again, dream of a silence, a dream silence, full of murmurs, I don't know, that's all words, never wake, all words, there's nothing else, you must go on, that's all I know, they're going to stop, I know that well, I can feel it, they're going to abandon me, it will be the silence, for a moment, a good few moments, or it will be mine, the lasting one, that didn't last, that still lasts, it will be I, you must go on, I can't go on, you must go on, I'll go on, you must say words, as long as there are any, until they find me, until they say me, strange pain, strange sin, you must go on, perhaps it's done already, perhaps they have said me already, perhaps they have carried me to the threshold of my story, before the door that opens on my own story, that would surprise me, if it opens, it will be I, it will be the silence, where I am, I don't know, I'll never know, in the silence you don't know, you must go on, I can't go on, I'll go on.
(*Trilogy*, 367-8, 372-3, 375-8, 380-2)

It's one of the most intense endings in modern literature. But of course it's not an ending. There can be no classical narrative closure to such nervous energy, to such epistemological fear and hermeneutic violence. No closure: instead a disturbing openness, a decentred, alienated desire, and the Beckett voice goes on prattling for another 36 years.

The s-i-l-e-n-c-e <<—>> s-p-e-e-c-h problem goes beyond being an artistic or philosophic one: it involves all of life for Samuel Beckett. It lies at the core of life for him, embedded within eating, sleeping and being. Artists such as Andrei Tarkovsky, Robert Bresson, Ingmar Bergman, John Cage and Karl Kraus have spoken passionately about silence. Two philosophers in particular have written interesting things about silence: Ludwig Wittgenstein (1889-1951) and Michel Foucault (1926-1984). In 1983, in an interview, Foucault said:

> I often wondered why people had to speak. Silence may be a much more interesting way of having a relationship with people... I think silence is one of those things that has unfortunately been dropped from our culture. We don't have a culture of silence. (4)

Certainly Samuel Beckett has helped to make silence a possibility again. So much of contemporary culture in radio/ TV/ magazines/ internet/ cel phones/ music/ art is vapid and trivial. There is so much useless babble in the world. One of the best lines in the Beckett's *Trilogy* says this:

> Not one person in a hundred knows how to be silent and listen, no, nor even to conceive what such a thing means. Yet only then can you detect, beyond the fatuous clamour, the silence of which the universe is made. (*Molloy*, T, 112)

Samuel Beckett's task is to push language to its limits. In doing so he often veers into mysticism, into a zone only inhabited by extremists who move beyond metaphysics, ontology and art. Charting the unknown areas of epistemology, the Austrian philosopher Ludwig Wittgenstein came up with some philosophical notions that would infuriate Beckett, as recorded in his *Tractatus Logicus-Philosophicus*

> Everything that can be put into words can be put clearly. (*Tractatus*, 26)

No, no, no, I can hear Samuel Beckett cry from the other side of Mount Olympus. That is not How It Is, he would say. But Ludwig Wittgenstein possessed pinpoint accuracy when it came to investigating language:

> 5.62 The world is *my* world: this is manifest in the fact that the limits of language... mean the limits of *my* world, (ib., 57)

Samuel Beckett would be in agreement here. The world, language and human experience become one. There are no absolutes. Instead, there is a total subjectivity completely dependent on the individual and the umpteen vicissitudes of life.

The most pertinent insight in *Tractatus Logicus-Philosophicus* is number 6.522:

> There are, indeed, things that cannot be put into words. They *make themselves manifest* They are what is mystical. (ib., 73)

Samuel Beckett works in this 'zone of being', where silence, art, language and nothingness merge. All these things (and more) are bound up together in Beckett's metaphysics, because his is a philosophy of opposites, an endless tautology, in which the opposite of any statement is also true. Therefore, silence implies speech, art indicates non-art, and underneath the mess/ chaos there must be nothingness. What Beckett does is to make chaos and nothingness, which are scientific/ religious concepts, real experiences.

Samuel Beckett is an artist, not a philosopher (indeed, he claimed he didn't understand philosophers: 'All I am is feeling' [L. Graver, 217]). His solutions are artistic ones, not philosophical ones.

Nevertheless, the number of times that Samuel Beckett's art corresponds with elements of mysticism, Existentialism, theology, Greek philosophy, Gnosticism, Buddhism, painting, cinema, music and so on, are beyond collation. The number of papers and books on Beckett and his art attest to this. But there is still much to be discussed.

For instance: Samuel Beckett's nothingness. What kind of void is it? Nothingness lies below the mystical centres of Buddhism and Christianity. There is in Tibetan Buddhism the 'Clear Light of the Void', a concept Beckett refers to indirectly in his white-on-white spaces of later texts pieces such as *Imagination Dead Imagine* and *Ping*. At this point, in the extreme zones of mysticism, words such as 'darkness' and 'void' and 'nothingness' and 'negation' merge. Clearly, the darkness that surrounds the dramatic space of much of Beckett's theatre is a kind of nothingness. Darkness is part of the chaos which is part of the nothingness.

Samuel Beckett attacks this central experiential zone in a number of ways. Sometimes it is a white space, or a black space, or a skull alone, or disembodied voices, or speech trailing into silences. 'In the last book, *L'Innommable*, there's complete disintegration', he said (in Israel Shenker, in L. Graver).

Samuel Beckett's nothingness is always experienced through a human personality. Even his most abstract of voices/ texts disseminates through human personalities. His derelicts have nothing, possess nothing, often desire nothing. Nothing happens in his plots. His art moves from nothingness to nothingness. Yet the nothingness is always a Something, Something experienced by some form of humanity. The impossibility of experiencing nothingness fascinates Beckett. 'Feeling nothing, knowing nothing, capable of nothing, wanting nothing', he wrote in *The Trilogy* (T, 320). This is the state of *nirvana*, the Buddhist heaven, desirelessness.

Renunciation is a key element in most mysticisms. In Samuel Beckett's poesie, as in mysticism, it is a way back to the Centre, to the self. Western mystics such as St John of the Cross, Walter Hilton, Richard of St Victor and Jesus have said how important it is to renounce worldly things. In *Texts For Nothing* (no. X), Beckett writes:

> No, no souls, or bodies, or birth, or life, or death, you've got to go on without any of that junk, that's all dead with words, with excess of words...
> (Prose, 105)

It's all junk but it's also the stuff of life. Samuel Beckett's characters and narrators try to transcend it. The first stage of transcendence is the negation of self, the dying-to-self of Christian mysticism. One has to transcend Heraclitean flux, the Buddhist *samsara*.

The next stage is the Dark Night of the Soul, which seems to be the perpetual state of Samuel Beckett's souls (the Dantean Purgatory). Perpetual limbo. Half-light. Confusion, doubt, uncertainty. Thus Beckett in his essay "Dante...Bruno. Vico....Joyce" wrote:

> Hell is the static lifelessness of unrelieved viciousness. Paradise the static lifelessness of unrelieved immaculation. Purgatory a flood of movement and vitality released by the conjunction of these two elements. (D, 33)

This is always Samuel Beckett's stance: never one thing or the other. This is why ecstasy/ *satori*/ enlightenment/ unity/ transcendence is never achieved. Unity is the aim of many mysticisms – Sufism, Taoism, Neoplatonism and Gnosticism – but it can never occur in Beckett's dialectical world.

The mystics most like Samuel Beckett are therefore those who speak of darkness/ nothingness/ renunciation/ strife/ negation: Meister

Eckhart, Jan van Ruysbroeck, St John of the Cross, Hui-Neng, etc. Jan van Ruysbroeck spoke of the 'inward man' entering 'into the God-seeing life' (F. Happold, 289), while Meister Eckhart (c. 1260-1328) evoked God in a way that Beckett would approve of:

> Love him as he is: a not-God, a not-spirit, a not-Person, a not-image; as sheer, pure, limpid unity, alien from all duality. And in this one let us sink down eternally from nothingness to nothingness. (ib., 274)

This is precisely what Samuel Beckett's texts do: they (try to) sink down, from nothingness to nothingness. Beckett said he sat at his table for two or three hours, so he could 'descend into the darkness' (quoted in H. Kenner, *Guide,* 184). The sinking-down is meditative, with correspondences in the contemplative traditions of Buddhism, Hinduism, Sufism, etc. Meister Eckhart, in his *Christmas Day Sermons,* spoke of this kind of ritualized, mystical introspection:

> To achieve the interior act one must assemble all one's powers as it were into one corner of one's soul, where, secreted from images and forms, one is able to work. In this silence, this quiet, the Word is heard. There is no better method of approaching this Word than in silence, in quiet... (F. Happold, 77)

This act of contemplation is found in most of Samuel Beckett's art: the woman in the play *Rockaby* rocks to and fro in a primal/ foetal/ sexual/ meditative way, while she listens to a voice out of the darkness. Beckett was aware of the religious allusions of the voice heard in darkness: he said he was thinking of St Jerome (the saint in the wilderness, a popular image in Renaissance art).

Dionysius the Areopagite (6th century) is a pre-Dantean mystic of descent and darkness. He spoke of a 'superessential Radiance' and 'divine Darkness' (F. Happold, 212). Darkness in Dionysius' cosmology is God's secret place (ib., 214). As in later treatises, such as the 14th century English text *The Cloud of Unknowing* and Meister Eckhart's sermons, language is strained to its limits: terms such as *superessential, unknowing, darkness* and *essence* are employed in a post-Neoplatonic mishmash of mysticism:

> We pray that we may come unto this Darkness which is beyond light, and, without seeing and without knowing, to see and to know that which is above vision and knowledge through the realization that by not-seeing and by unknowing we attain to true vision and knowledge. (*The Mystical Theology*, in ib., 214)

The links between Samuel Beckett and Dionysius the Areopagite are strengthened due to Dionysius' writings on the angelic hierarchies, which influenced Dante Alighieri's poetic vision of Paradise.

One way to define nothingness/ darkness/ silence is to say everything it *isn't*. This is the 'not-this-not-that' realm of Oriental mysticism. Thus the *Heart Sutra* of Buddhism describes emptiness in ways wholly in tune with Beckett's vision:

> in emptiness there is no form, nor feeling, nor perception, nor impulse, nor consciousness; no eye, ear, nose, tongue, body, mind; no forms, sounds, smells, tastes, touchables, objects of mind; no sight-organ-element, and so forth, until we come to: no mind-consciousness-element; there is no ignorance, no extinction of ignorance, and so forth, until we come to: there is no decay and death, no extinction of decay and death; there is no suffering, no origination, no stopping, no path; there is no cognition, no attainment, and no non-attainment. (in F. Happold, 162-3)

Although Samuel Barclay Beckett occasionally wrote a string of *no's*, or negatives, he was never as severe as this. One of the fundamental differences between Eastern and Western mysticism (and ideology) is the Oriental emphasis on the extinction of the ego. The West exalts the ego, and ego-annihilation is often too hideous to contemplate. Thus in Beckett's *The Unnamable*, his most extreme text, the voice or self still has a personality, a sort of body, and a spatial context. The Buddhist realm, as portrayed in the *Heart Sutra*, takes phenomenological austerity to its extreme. The Western world is so sensuous in comparison (think of Henry Vaughan's superdazzling darkness, the Night of Novalis, the star-filled skies of Heinrich Heine and Thomas Hardy, and the æsthetic/ tragic renunciations of Friedrich Nietzsche and Arthur Schopenhauer).

The *via negativa* (the converse of the *via affirmativa* or *via illuminativa*) is Samuel Beckett's way. Dionysius the Areopagite is one of the principle 'negative way' mystics of the West. The tendency towards silence was there in Beckett's earliest works. In *Proust* he wrote:

> For the artist who does not deal in surfaces, the rejection of friendship is not only reasonable, but a necessity. Because the only possible spiritual development is in the sense of depth, the artistic tendency is not expansive, but a contraction. And art is the apotheosis of solitude. (Proust, 64)

In Samuel Beckett's literary philosophy, the negation often manifests itself as hyper-self-consciousness. Beckett takes self-reflexivity to extremes. He comments upon the narrative as it's being shaped. He retracts statements, contradicts himself, produces multiplitic mirror effects. There is a voice behind each voice, and another voice behind that one. Fictions multiply. The Unnamable renounces his story as he goes along. He rejects previous versions (Mahood, Molloy, etc).

The self-awareness of/ in Samuel Beckett's art is part of his thesis/ antithesis view of the world. Eternal dualism. The self-reflexivity and *mise-en-âbyme* gives Beckett's art a peculiar character, and his narrators become intimate confiders of failure. As in the art of Marcel Duchamp and Robert Rauschenberg, Beckett's art rejects artifice, while simultaneously acknowledging that it is all artifice.

The paradoxes breed, and Samuel Beckett loves them. The art/ non-art dialectic is one more to add to the long list of Beckettian dichotomies and struggles. In the lyrical late piece *Ill Seen, Ill Said* (1981), Beckett makes constant references to the manufacture of the work itself:

> Nothing left but black sky. White earth. Or inversely. No more sky or earth. Finished high and low. Nothing but black and white. Everywhere no matter where. But black. Void. Nothing else. Contemplate that. (Ill, 31)

The problem with self-reflexivity is that diegetic effect can be ruined to the point where only superficial polemics can be communicated. But Beckett keeps the alienating tendency in check by including it as part of the narrator's self-questioning.

The irony is that although Samuel Beckett (or his narrator) has nothing to express and nothing with which to express, he nevertheless carries on expressing. The composer John Cage put it thus:

> Our poetry now is the realization that we possess nothing... I have nothing to say and I am saying it and that is poetry as I need it. (109-110)

An artist with no subject matter, no forms, and nothing to say, Samuel Beckett even so finds many things to discuss, many different forms for his messages, and has a good deal to say. Part of the delight of Beckett's art is that he starts with nothing. Or rather, with everything, and reduces it to nothing. Hamm trains the telescope outside in the play *Endgame* and sees 'Zero... (*he looks*)... zero... (*he looks*)... and zero.' Hamm replies: 'Nothing stirs.' (Works, 106)

Samuel Beckett's derelicts try to say the Unsay-able; they try to do the Undo-able and be the Unbe-able. They fail, which is the least (or the most) they expect. Beckett takes platitudes such as 'nothing gained, nothing win', 'he who dares, wins', 'fortune favours the bold', and 'no harm trying', and pulverizes them. He creates an empire of failure, in which the crowned emperor is the one who fails the best. Depth, not expansion, as he said in *Proust*.

Certainly the vertical axis in Samuel Beckett's art is the one most often explored. A pole between Heaven and Hell: ascension is nearly impossible: descent is much more common. But Purgatory is the best place to be, of the three.

The strength to ascend/ transcend is beyond most of Samuel Beckett's people: they must be content/ discontent with the eternal push-and-pull conflict of an in-between zone, somewhere between yes and no, a Land of Maybe.

The in-between zone, the 'zone of being', the 'zone of stones' of *Ill Seen Ill Said* (Ill, 9), is Samuel Beckett's longed-for place, a Purgatory of unending flux. Here, there is no victor in the struggle between presence and absence. And it is very dark.

Few writers have made more of darkness than Samuel Beckett. In *Endgame* we hear that Mother Pegg died of darkness (Works, 129); in *Play* (1963), W1 opens the speech thus:

> Yes, strange, darkness best, and the darker the worse, till all dark, then all

well (ib., 307)

In ...*but the clouds*... (1976), M's voice speaks of

crouching there, in my little sanctum, in the dark (ib., 422)

In *A Piece of Monologue* (1980), Beckett goes back over his birth:

Nothing. Empty dark. Till first word always the same. Night after night the same. Birth. Then slowly fade up of a faint form. Out of the dark. (ib., 427)

We have to add birth and the womb to the poetic correspondences already pointed out between silence/ speech/ art/ nothingness/ chaos/ death/ time/ being, etc.

Samuel Beckett's art sinks into the darkness as much as into the silence. In the works of the middle period (*Waiting For Godot*, *The Molloy Trilogy*), the darkness is often feared: it is the cruel void, giving back nothing. In the late works, particularly in the poetic trilogy *Company, Ill Seen, Ill Said* and *Worstward Ho*, the darkness becomes sensual, restful, nourishing even, something more akin to the darkness of the poetry of Henry Vaughan, Friedrich Hölderlin, Arthur Rimbaud and Paul Verlaine, and Novalis in his *Hymns to the Night*:

Night's rule is timeless
And spaceless. –
Forever
Is the length of sleep
Holy sleep. (22)

In *Company* (1980), the darkness is sometimes described in sensuous terms, and the narrator embraces it. The anger and violence of *How It Is* and *Texts For Nothing* is tempered by a resignation and acquiescence. These later texts are more circumspect, more thoughtful. The flood of words is curtailed in favour of a dense, post-Symbolist economy and precision, reminiscent of the poesie of Paul Verlaine and Stéphane Mallarmé.

In the late works, fiction and drama, there is a continuous

evocation of light failing, dimming, fading to black. It is one of the most magical components of Samuel Beckett's drama, this slow fading to black (in *Footfalls* and *Rockaby*, for instance). Beckett's obsession with lighting is startling. Reading the plays, one is struck by the precision of the lighting directions (in *Play* and *Quad*, for example). The interplay between light and dark fascinates Beckett. If he mentions anything of a scene, he notes the lighting. He is a very visually-aware writer, and his visuals always consist of lighting first and foremost. In his 1961 interview with Tom Driver, he said:

> If life and death did not both present themselves to us, there would be no inscrutability. If there were only darkness, all would be clear. It is because there is not only darkness but also light that our situation becomes inexplicable. (in L. Graver, 220)

Samuel Beckett's concern is with the mystery of dualism, not the Zorasterian/ Manichean/ Gnostic allusions of the mystery: though in many ways Gnostic, as we have said, Beckett's notions transcend philosophy because they are grounded in direct human experience (not instituionalized or organized versions of those experiences). The light/ dark dichotomy fascinates him because it is already there; it is a 'given', in and for itself. Words do not alter the light/ dark cycle, but the light/ dark phenomena severely alters the fiction. Without it Beckett's art would be radically different. The light/ dark syndrome is at the base of his work. *Company*, among many other texts, begins and ends with the darkness. Darkness is woven into Beckett's texts not as manifestation/ presentation/ analysis, but as a Prime Mover, an already-given, the stuff that existed before the Creation, before Time, before the Big Bang, before God.

In *Company* there are many evocations and experiences of darkness:

> A voice comes to one in the dark. Imagine... As in shadow he lay and only the odd sound slowly silence fell and darkness gathered... Dark lightens while it sounds. Deepens while it ebbs... To let in and shut out the dark... Who asks who exclaims. What visions in the shadeless dark of light and shade... The fable of one with you in the dark. The fable of one fabling of one with you in the dark. And how better in the end labour lost and silence.

And you as you always were. Alone. (C, 7, 23, 25, 37, 84, 88-89)

The darkness in Samuel Beckett's art functions in many ways: it is, partly, a means of interrogating the 'zones of being' at the core of life; it is also a device of fiction which corresponds so well to a psychic state (an ancient correspondence); it is also a way of actualizing the zones of void and silence which have been Beckett's artistic province since *The Trilogy*.

In *Worstward Ho* (1983), he makes more references to the void than ever before. It is foregrounded as a soul-space of half-language/ half-experience. Only language takes us there; only language can bring us back:

> The dim. The void... No ground. Plod as on void... On back to unsay void can go. Void cannot go... From the void. From the stare. In the skull all save the skull gone. The stare. Alone in the dim void... Longing that all go. Dim go. Void go. Longing go. Vain longing go. Vain longing that vain longing go... Less. Less seen. Less seeing. Less seen and seeing when with with words than when not... All save void. No, void too. Unworsenable void. Never less. Never first. Never more. Never since first said never unsaid never worse said never not gnawing to be gone

(Who, 14, 16, 18, 25, 36, 39, 42)

These late texts seem to be Samuel Beckett at his finest. They are successful on many counts. They succeed because:

(1) they are not overlong, like *The Unnamable*, which was over-the-top;

(2) They are highly poetic;

(3) they weave in autobiography;

(4) they are self-reflexive;

(5) they quest/ question;

(6) they enjoy wordplay;

(7) they have a fluidity of time and space;

(8) they transcend any notion of 'literary influences';

(9) they are self-subsisting, with no need for explication or comparison;

and (10) they have a clarity which Francesco Petrarch, Gustave

Flaubert and James Joyce would admire.

Samuel Beckett has streamlined his style so that he keeps a tighter hold on meanings than in earlier works. He does this by using a restrained syntax and punctuation. In *How It Is,* he used no punctuation other than spaces; in *The Unnamable,* he employed the comma excessively. In the three late *Nohow On* works, punctuation is simple and direct: the full stop, employed to end short, simple sentences, many of them just phrases. While the internal references might multiply, the outward effect is of a sparse and clean text, a fiction that comes close to Gustave Flaubert's ideal book – one that has had all the extraneous material stripped away – 'a book about nothing' (M. Allott, 242).

Sam Beckett doesn't achieve linguistic transparency (is that possible?), but he gets close. The later works come closest to Beckett's dictum (*pace* James Joyce) that 'form is content, content is form' ("Dante... Bruno. Vico... Joyce" [D, 27]). Here, Beckett's texts have a sculptural form, a purity of line as found in the sculptures of Jean Arp and Constantin Brancusi.

Visual and syntactic purity combine in Samuel Beckett's texts: the sparseness runs through his form, content and subject matter, in terms of the older, humanist criticism. In terms of the newer cultural theory, Beckett's texts, meta-texts, signifieds, surfaces, metaphors, *mise-en-scène, mise-en-âbyme,* self-reflexivity, structures, politics and images have an amazingly powerful sense of unity.

The analogies with painting are useful: Samuel Beckett's love of pure, hard lines and blacks/ whites recalls all manner of printing techniques; Thomas Hardy admired J.M.W. Turner in this respect; and Beckett's short texts of the 1960s and 1970s have correspondences in 1960s Minimal, Colorfield and Hard Edge painting, in the art of painters such as Barnett Newman, Frank Stella and Brice Marden. The contemporary art movements of Minimalism, Non-Relationalism, Non-Gestural Art, Abstract Mannerism, Systematic Painting and Colorfield Painting have correspondences with Beckett's visual and syntactic structures.

Like the painters of the contemporary period, Samuel Beckett uses seriality, presence/ absence, hard edges, non-objectivity, intense subjectivity, mythic/ tragic themes, post-Existential angst, self-reflexivity, occultisms such as numerology and astrology, Minimal gestures, and all kinds of abstraction.

Samuel Beckett's theatrical spaces could easily double as environmental or installation art in a New York City art gallery. Texts such as *Ping* and *Imagination Dead Imagine* have equivalents in the white-on-white paintings of Robert Ryman, in the abstract, geometrical art of Sol LeWitt, or Agnes Martin's pencilled squares, faint, grey, dreamy, void-like. The blocks and cubes of Carl Andre, Richard Serra, Robert Morris and David Smith are the 3-D versions of Beckett's claustrophic spaces. The evocations in Beckett's works of emptiness, of deserts or vast, white environments are analogous with the epic canvases of Mark Rothko, Morris Louis and Robert Motherwell.

The artist Géorges Baziotes has described his goal in Beckettian terms:

> It is the mysteriousness that I love in painting... It is the stillness and the silence. I want my pictures to take effect very slowly, to obsess and to haunt. (In M. Tuchman, *The New York School* 45).

This is two passages from *Ping*, an evocation a white body in a white space:

> Given rose only just bare white body fixed one yard white on white invisible. All white all known murmurs only just almost never always the same all known. Light heat hands hanging palms front white on white invisible. Bare white body fixed ping elsewhere. [...}
> Eyes holes light blue alone uncover given blue light blue almost white only colour fixed front. All white all known white planes shining white ping murmur only just almost never one second light time that much memory almost never. Bare white body fixed one yard ping fixed elsewhere white on white invisible heart breath no sound. (Prose, 149-150)

The brutal circumscription of this white environment corresponds with the empty gallery that the French modern artist Yves Klein exhibited, with one of Duane Hanson's painted dummies in it. In the 1960s the art object assumed a primacy: the inside became outside.

Contemporary painting is a mass of contradictions: it is abstract yet real/ unreal; it is non-figurative yet constantly speaks of/ to the human individual; it is unconscious but highly self-conscious; it is non-gestural, but always gestural; it is non-objective, yet very metaphysical, etc.

One painter in particular seems to have many parallels with Samuel Beckett: Ad Reinhardt (1913-1967), who may be called, in the terminology of the era, a post-painterly meta-structural non-objective super-mystical neo-abstractionist. Reinhardt spent the Sixties painting black, five-foot square canvases again and again in a studio in New York City. He kept reducing his art until there was nothing left but a black square – far away from Kasimir Malevich's black square. Reinhardt's aim was:

> No lines or imaginings, no shapes or composings or representations, no visions or sensations or impulses, no symbols or signs or impastos, no decoratings or colourings or picturings, no pleasures or pains, no accidents or readymades, no things, no ideas, no relations, no attributes, no qualities – nothing that is not of 'the essence'. ("Art=as=Art", 1960)

The goal comes from Buddhism. In Samuel Beckett's art we find similar statements of negation. Ad Reinhardt failed, of course. It turns out that his paintings, each one entitled *Abstract Painting, Black*, were relational/ representational/ visionary. He could not erase the human mark. In some ways, Reinhardt's paintings are the last in the Western/ Renaissance mode: the End of Painting, as he intended. His paintings aimed to be the last ever made, but as Jasper Johns so rightly noted: 'A lot of people have said that painting is dead, but people continue to work' (in E. de Antonio, 163). Painting is not dead, neither is writing. As Ad Reinhardt and Beckett have demonstrated, you can go on refining for ever. Art is endless. Despite the (typically masculinist) wish for obliteration, for a total dissolution in chaos, people continue to create.

Ad Reinhardt reached a dead-end: the repetition of the same image, over and over; Samuel Beckett's repetition allows for much more variation. But there is the same sense of hacking away at the same image or text, again and again. Painters such as J.M.W. Turner, Mark

Rothko, Vincent van Gogh and Georges Rouault seem to have painted one picture endlessly. The same can be said of writers such as Henry Miller, James Joyce, Emily Dickinson, Francesco Petrarch, Raymond Carver and D.H. Lawrence, tackling the same subject repeatedly.

In the work of Samuel Beckett, repetition is musical and mystical. His mantra-like phrases sink into the senses deeply. Like many powerful authors (such as Arthur Rimbaud, William Shakespeare, Emily Brontë), Beckett works on all of the reader's senses (the five senses, plus time, plus the sixth sense of occultism/ the paranormal).

The visual aspects of Samuel Beckett's art have been well-documented by many critics: the many references to painters; the discussions of painting in several essays; the painterly concern for form, design, space and lighting. Painters of darkness, such as Jan Vermeer, Leonardo da Vinci, Emil Nolde, Georges Rouault and Odilon Redon, are the obvious comparisons; as are the Expressionist artists, such as Egon Schiele with his twisted, tormented bodies, or Max Beckmann with his triptychs of pain and social injustices. Idiosyncratic/ individualistic artists such as Paul Klee, Henri Matisse, Alberto Giacometti, James Ensor and Wassily Kandinsky touch on Beckett's art at many points. One thinks of the tragic clowns of Rouault, the tortured Christs of Lovis Corinth and Nolde, the cities as Infernos of Otto Dix, Edvard Munch's wan, pained souls, or Chaim Soutine's highly-charged portraits.

Certainly Samuel Beckett's texts have the savagery of Georges Grosz or Otto Dix – the portrait of the human being in which every flaw is ruthlessly exposed. The connections with the modern, European Expressionists are deep: one recalls how Beckett was concerned early on with expression, and how difficult the whole enterprise is/ can be/ must be.

Samuel Beckett's production notebooks are peppered with doodles – usually of people, characters perhaps, from his plays. The visual impact of the drama is meticulously planned. But what is the typical Beckettian situation?

A track; a swamp; a desert; a plain; hills; a forest; a sea shore; cloudy light usually; often night; often raining; sometimes snow; seldom bright sunlight; distinctly Northern, not Mediterranean/ Asian/ Russian/ American, etc; a hat; a long coat; boots; rocking chairs; a bike; a stick; crutches; a cave/ hut/ house/ apartment/ street/ a park; a park bench.

A typical setting is a windswept strand: the protagonist is alone amidst the vastness. This early Beckett poem depicts the scene succinctly:

> encore le dernier reflux
> le galet mort
> le demi-tour puis le pas
> vers les vieilles lumières
>
> (again the last ebb
> the dead shingle
> the turning then the steps
> towards the lights
> of old) (Poems, 50-51)

It recalls the poet in Heinrich Heine's *The North Sea* cycle (1825-26):

> On the wan shore of the sea
>   Lonely I sat with troubled thoughts.
>   The sun dropped lower, and cast
>   Glowing red streaks on the water. ('Twilight')

In *Company* the scene is replayed for the *n*-th time (and one of the last times):

> A strand. Evening. Light dying. Soon none left to die. No. No such thing then as no light. Died on to dawn and never died. You stand with your back to the wash. No sound but its. Ever fainter as it slowly ebbs. Till it slowly flows again. You lean on a long staff. Your hands rest on the knob and on them your head. Were your eyes to open they would first see far below in the last rays the skirt of your greatcoat and the uppers of your boots emerging from the sand. Then and it alone till it vanishes the shadow of the staff on the sand. Vanishes from your sight. Moonless starless night. Were your eyes to open dark would lighten. (C, 76)

A clichéd poetic scenario here; a typical self-referentiality; an emphasis on the imagination and its power/ powerlessness to make life; a sense of the mnemonic; and the precise use of the second-person voice.

This is one of Samuel Beckett's major settings: a sad, stony beach in Northern Europe: the North Sea/ Irish Sea/ Atlantic Ocean. The wide-open space functions to isolate the individual: the soul-space is both inner and outer, echoing too the surface of emptiness in the text. Variations include the grey desert of *Lessness* , here quoted in both languages:

> Ruines répandues confondues avec le sable gris cendre vrai réfuge. Cube tout lumière blancheur rase faces sans trace aucun souvenir. Jamais ne fut qu'air gris sans temps chimère lumière qui passe. Gris cendre ciel reflet de la terre reflet du ciel. Jamais ne fut que cet inchangeant rêve l'heure qui passe.
>
> Scattered ruins same grey as the sand ash grey true refuge. Pour square all light sheer white blank planes all gone from mind. Never was but grey air timeless no sound figment the passing light. No sound no stir ash grey mirrored earth mirrored sky. Never but this changelessness dream the passing hour. (*Têtes-Mortes*, 69; Prose, 153)

The French language brings out the poetry of the text in a different way: more internal rime and alliteration. The scene, evoked in a dense, highly compressed style, echoes that strain of French poetry of which Charles Baudelaire and Paul Verlaine are typical representatives. In *How It Is* we hear of the 'warmth of primeval mud impenetrable dark' (12), a more extreme version of the countryside of *Waiting For Godot* with its twisted, Alberto Giacometti tree. In *The Trilogy* the landscape is recognisably that of Beckett's Irish childhood:

> From there he must have seen it all, the plain, the sea, and then these selfsame hills that some call mountains, indigo in places in the evening light, their serried ranges crowding to the skyline, cloven with hidden valleys that the eye divines from sudden shifts of colour and then from other signs for which there are no words, nor even thoughts. (Molloy, T, 11)

Here's a rarity: a colour other than black or white: indigo. Samuel Beckett's palette is loaded with a variety of blacks (ebony, sable, lamp), and a smattering of whites (zinc, lead, flake, chalk), but very few colours. Blue appears occasionally for someone's eyes. Other colours are very rare, except for grey. Beckett has more blacks than Diego Velásquez or Francisco de Zurbáran, the blackest of Spanish painters. Within his limited range of colouration, Beckett provides many startling images. He uses lighting changes, often described in a practical tone, as if he's giving notes to a lighting technician for a theatrical production. This example is typical of Beckett's control of lighting, from the vicious text *All Strange Away* (1979):

> Black cold any length, then light slow up to full glare say ten seconds still and hot glare any length all ivory white all six planes no shadow, then down through deepening greys and gone, so on. (Prose, 121)

If you compare this extract with the lighting directions for the play *Rockaby*, you see how close Beckett's fiction and drama is: the imagery, symbolism, sense of space (and time) are often one:

> Light: subdued on chair. Rest of stage dark. Subdued spot on face constant throughout, unaffected by successive fades. Either wide enough to include narrow limits of rock or concentrated on face when still or at mid-rock. Then throughout speech face slightly swaying in and out of light. Opening fade-up: first spot on face alone, long pause, then light on chair. Final fade-out: first chair, long pause with spot on face alone, head slowly sinks, come to rest, fade out spot. (Works, 433)

Clearly Samuel Beckett enjoys the problems set by technical/ mathematical explorations of spaces. So many of his texts pivot on mathematically precise descriptions of spaces, whether they be boats, stone rings, huts or boxes.

Spaces need illumination, and however much he loves to sink into the darkness, Samuel Beckett must always use illumination. Often Beckett will state that a place was black/ dark, and then contradict himself (in *Company* and *Worstward Ho*, for instance). He can't be content with all-black or all-white. This is part of his thesis/ antithesis turn of mind. His fear of total blackness is a manifestation of that Western clinging onto the ego, that terror of losing the self. So the nearblackness, like the near-silence, is a compromise in which a little of humanity can remain. An Oriental artist might erase that glimmer completely (the Orient's extinction of the ego). For Beckett this is too much. He must always retain some semblance of the self.

White is the flipside of black, and Samuel Beckett often moves from extreme to extreme. Thus he writes in the radio play *From an Abandoned Work* (1957):

> White I must say has always affected me strongly, all white things, sheets, walls and so on, even flowers, and then just white, the thought of white, without more. (Prose, 131)

Among modern writers, only D.H. Lawrence seems to have been obsessed with white to such a degree. The all-white space recalls the asylum, the hospital, the sanitorium, the obliteration of the *Tibetan Book of the Dead*. In some ways, all-white zones are more terrifying than all-black ones (as some science-fiction novels and movies have explored).

Taken to artistic extremes, the white-on-white spatial descriptions do tend towards religiosity – in their longing for obliteration. The whitescapes of *Ping* and *Imagination Dead Imagine* are the most oppressive in Sam Beckett's texts. This is from the latter:

> Go back out, move back, the little fabric vanishes, ascend, it vanishes, all white in the whiteness, descend, go back in. Emptiness, silence, heat, whiteness, wait, the light goes down, all grows dark together, ground, wall, vault, bodies, say twenty seconds, all the greys, the light goes out, all vanishes. (Prose, 145)

This is not the brilliance of (religious) revelation. Ecstasy is rare in Sam Beckett's art, unlike in that of D.H. Lawrence or Hermann Hesse. The revelation on the pier in Dublin is a one-off; the reverberations of it are only dimly glimpsed in Beckett's postwar works. The word 'dazzling' occurs in *Company* (52), which is the only time I've seen it in Beckett's art.

In a variety of ways a Samuel Beckett protagonist goes back over some earlier, brighter time in their life. The light of memory contrasts painfully with the darkness of the present. The contrasts are never resolved into one tone, one colour, black or white. There are no absolutes, only a fretful shuttling back and forth. There was light once, as the narrator of *Company* explains:

> The light there was then. On your back in the dark the light there was then. Sunless cloudless brightness. You slip away at break of day and climb to your hiding place on the hillside. A nook in the gorse. East beyond the sea the faint shape of high mountain. Seventy miles away according to your Longman. For the third or fourth time in your life. The first time you told them and were derided. All you had seen was cloud. So now you hoard it in your heart with the rest. Back home at nightfall supperless to bed.
>
> You lie in the dark and are back in that light. Straining out from your nest in the gorse with your eyes across the water till they ache. You close them while you count a hundred. Then open and strain again. Again and again. Till in the end it is there. Palest blue against the pale sky. You lie in the dark and are back in that light. Fall asleep in that sunless cloudless light. Sleep till morning light. (C, 32-34)

This is a late example of Samuel Beckett's occasional moments of nature mysticism. He hates poetic pantheism, the Wordsworthian exaltation of nature. But the natural world is one of the consolations of the Beckettian anti-hero when s/he is pausing a moment in the pursuit of solitude and darkness and silence.

Compared to poets such as Heinrich Heine, Johann Wolfgang von Goethe, Percy Shelley or Alexander Pushkin, Beckett's nature mysticism is extremely restrained. Yet it is there, in the sunset of *Still*, in Molloy toiling across the Irish plains, in the stone circle of *Ill Seen Ill Said*, even in the Giacomettian tree of *Waiting For Godot*.

Samuel Beckett might over-state negatives, but not affirmations. He has said, and this explains a lot, that 'the slightest eloquence becomes unbearable' (L. Harvey, 249). So his evocations of nature border on the mundane. Sometimes he is as matter-of-fact as a police report. And yet the poetry shines through (Beckett cannot help being eloquent, or poetic, even if it's the poetry of minimalism). In the *Four Novellas/ Stories* (1977), for instance, where the derelict shuffles from basement to cave to boat, he notes the sky, earth, weather, animals, flowers, etc. Beckett may be sparse, but the elements still rage there. There is wind, rain and snow in Beckett's art in great quantities. The typical Beckettian landscape, the 'ruinstrewn land' of *Afar a Bird* (Prose, 195), is not barren but nourishing. This is, after all, where the Beckett derelicts wish to be. The landscape is both loved and hated, a refuge, an escape, as well as a lonely prison.

The landscape is a constant source of delight and frustration in the texts of Samuel Beckett. Take the tree in *Waiting For Godot*, which sprouts leaves despite being twisted like a Giacometti sculpture; but it is not strong enough to take someone hanging on it (the true test of the strength of a tree in Beckettland!). The anti-heroes of *The Trilogy* stagger through an arid world: 'dead world, airless, waterless' (in *Malone Dies*, T, 185). Yet they chose to be there.

Samuel Beckett's fictional landscapes are mediated through memory. They are not directly experienced. His texts are related by narrators, who constantly compare past and present. If landscape is featured, it is (nearly always) the memory of a landscape. In Beckett's art, we are (always) one step away from so-called 'reality'. There is a landscape; it's in the past; there is the subjective memory of it; then the description of it in words, by a narrator; then our reading of those words (and there are further layers, of course, as examined in reader theory). There are, thus, many veils, layers and levels of meaning and significance and value to pierce in Beckett's *œuvre*. His landscapes hover somewhere between ideality and reality, between experience and memory, between actuality and artifice.

A typical symbol of this mnemonic mediation is the window: characters have a window that looks out onto a landscape. 'the single window giving on outer dark' in *Company* (30), the sunset window in *Still*, or the Kensington window in *Murphy* (1938):

> There was not much light, the room devoured it, but she kept her face turned to what there was. The small single window condensed its changes, as half-closed eyes see the finer values of tones, so that it was never quiet in the room, but brightening and darkening in a slow ample flicker that went on all day, brightening against the darkening that was its end. A peristasis of light, worming its way into the dark. (M, 42)

This quiet contemplation of lighting of course mirrors the author at his/ her writing table, looking out of the window. Similarly, the remembrances of hot skies or particular landscapes stems from the writer's experience of writing. Samuel Beckett is no different from other authors who weave the dreamstuff of their texts out of their thoughts, so the Flesh becomes the Word, neatly reversing the thrust of religion.

To sum up some of Samuel Beckett's conflicts and dualities:
- speech/ silence,
- light/ dark,
- imagination/ death,
- love/ hate,
- solitude/ company,
- presence/ absence,
- art/ life,
- present/ past,
- desire/ non-desire,
- less/ more
- everything/ nothing,
- landscape/ void.

The ontological restlessness might be a part of modernist literature from late Thomas Hardy onwards, but in fact it is found in the work of William Shakespeare, in Petronius, and in Homer. Modernism merely talks about restlessness *ad nauseam*, making it the main discourse (*The Rainbow, The Stranger, Mysteries, Nausea, To The Lighthouse*, etc).

In *Mercier and Camier* (1946) comes the split of the Beckettian hero into two, the double act (straight man and gag man), the push-me-pull-you, the systole-diastole, the light/ dark, hot/ cold, ego/ shadow conflicts made actual. The split into two creates endless possibilities for dialogue, as *Waiting For Godot* and *Endgame* demonstrate. In *Mercier and Camier* rifts force the two apart, although they always seem to be together. The escape into landscape is not much of a refuge, either:

> In the end, he said, I am Mercier, alone, ill, in the cold, the wet, old, half mad, no way on, no way back. He eyed briefly, with nostalgia, the ghastly sky, the hideous earth. At your age, he said. Another act. Immaterial. (MC, 62)

In *More Pricks Than Kicks* (1934), the landscape veers from being a 'land of sanctuary' (27) to a post-Romantic, pastoral cliché:

> the grass was spangled with scarlet after-births, the larks were singing, the hedges were breaking, the sun was shining, the sky was Mary's cloak. (109)

Typical of Samuel Beckett to imagine a countryside strewn with afterbirths, an image both pastoral and Existential.

As in the writings of Johann Wolfgang von Goethe, Novalis and much of Romanticism, the time of day most eulogized in Samuel Beckett is dusk and night. There are umpteen sundowns in Beckett's texts as there are in D.H. Lawrence's works. A character widely awake in deep night is a common element. Molloy is a nature man who languishes in the noises one can hear at night:

> And that night there was no question of moon, nor any other light, but it was a night of listening, a night given to the faint soughing and sighing stirring at night in little pleasure gardens, the shy sabbath of leaves and petals and the air that eddies there as it does not in other places... (*Molloy*, T, 46)

In *The Unnamable* and *Texts For Nothing*, night becomes unbearable at times: 'this impossible night' says the narrator of *Text XII* (Prose, 111). By the time of fizzles such as *For To End Yet Again*, the inside night of the skull and the outer void have become interchangeable.

An offshoot of Samuel Beckett's immersion in the night is astronomy. Beckett's void is seldom utterly empty. In his clever wordplay he allows himself to qualify the word 'void', such as in *Worstward Ho*, where he writes 'the dim void' (25). But a void cannot be 'dim' or anything else but a void (as Buddhism states, and science knows). Always void. Void and nothing but void.

Look up at the night sky and you see it's teeming with life. The narrator of *Malone Dies* notes this, speaking of 'the nocturnal sky where nothing happens, though it is full of tumult and violence' (T, 218). It's the hostile, indifferent and Godless universe of Woody Allen, which doesn't care a jot about *you*.

Sam Beckett enjoys the Dantean vision of the cosmos, which is both mechanistic and divine, distinctly pre-Copernicus, pre-Galileo, pre-Newton, even though his universe has more in common with Albert Einstein, relativity, quantum theory and the New Physics.

If Dante Alighieri is one source of Samuel Beckett's astrophysical insights, the other must be James Joyce, particularly his 'ugly duckling' science sequence in 'Ithaca' in *Ulysses*:

> of Sirius (alpha in Canis Major) 10 light-years (57,000,000,000,000 miles) distant and in volume 900 times the dimension of our planet: of Arcturus: of the precession of the equinoxes: of Orion with belt and sextuple sun theta and nebula in which 100 of our solar systems could be contained... (*Ulysses*, 619)

The obsessive listing/ collation/ description of astronomical data in James Joyce's work appears in Samuel Beckett's texts as a musing upon his eternal themes of presence/ absence, solitude/ companionship, and life/ death. The stars seem to be static but are in motion; nothing seems to happen up there, but the sky is full of violence; and even the void is sprinkled with stars. These are the post-poetic thoughts which astronomy induces in Beckett's people, such as the object of the narrator's love in *Enough* (1966):

> In order from time to time to enjoy the sky he resorted to a little round mirror. Having misted it with his breath and polished it on his calf he looked in it for constellations. I have it! he exclaimed referring to the Lyre or the Swan. And often he added that the sky seemed much the same. (Prose, 142)

In their fashion, most of Samuel Beckett's derelicts are star-gazers (Watt, Molloy, Belacqua, Murphy). In his first novel, *Dream of Fair To Middling Women* (1932), Beckett writes lyrically of the celestial heavens: 'the night firmament is abstract density of music, symphony without end, illumination without end' (D, 44). This kind of pseudo-poetry, like T.S. Eliot *circa The Four Quartets* on a bad day, must be rejected. In one of Beckett's last fictions, the astronomy is skillfully and authentically interwoven with the text.

Ill Seen Ill Said is set in a stone circle, the 'zone of stones', presided over by twelve monoliths. The connotations are of rituals, astral geometry, prophecy, magic, the cycle of the seasons, the past, and so on. Clearly the old woman in *Ill Seen Ill Said* is a crone figure, the Goddess in her death/ Winter aspect, Hecate/ Cerrridwen/ Anne/

Hera/ Diana, the Black Goddess of Wisdom of Robert Graves. Much is made of circles: the stone ring, the dances of the stones, cycles, orbits, orbs of planets/ suns/ moons, zeroes and O's (in words such as 'moon', 'brood', 'doomed'), etc. The text opens with a sky ritual:

> From where she lies she sees Venus rise. From where she lies when the skies are clear she sees Venus rise followed by the sun. Then she rails at the source of all life. On. At evening when the skies are clear she savours its star's revenge. At the other window. Rigid upright on her old chair she watches for the radiant one. Her old deal spindlebacked chair. It emerges from out the last rays and sinking ever brighter is engulfed in its turn. On. She sits on erect and rigid in the deepening gloom. (7)

This passage contains many of Samuel Beckett's motifs: self-reflexivity ('On') and a reference to creation; the chair; voyeurism, and staring out of a window; rhythm of day/ night, light/ dark; ontological/ religious anger ('she rails at the source of all life'); enclosed space; the anonymous/ general (no names/ places/ dates); timelessness; and being trapped ('Rigid upright').

The stars/ sky/ nature/ elements form one kind of escape, one way of balancing up the unfair equations of the human condition. The odds are against us, the Beckettian anti-hero proclaims, but look at the stars, they are not troubled.

For the writer, talking about stars alleviates the pressure of the narrative for a few moments. The viewpoint suddenly changes, and events gain a new, cosmological perspective. Taken to its extreme, this cosmic perspective makes humanity dwindle into insignificance, next to the birth and death of gigantic suns, for instance.

Samuel Beckett's more common method of usurping the stress of the human condition is to sidestep life by using humour, or sex. Humour is strangely lacking in the diegetic worlds of the late texts, in *Company*, *Ill Seen Ill Said* and *Worstward Ho*, and there is little humour in texts such as *All Strange Away* and *The Lost Ones* Humour in these later works comes from the telling of the tale/ text; it is there in the author's oh-so-funny asides, in the choice of words. A Beckett text without humour is inauthentic, because in Beckett's work, humour is one of the hallmarks of an authentic response to life.

Samuel Beckett's humour ranges from wordplay to jokes to rage 'n' rants to absurdities such as sex, money, death, time, and memory. Beckett's jokes are often very funny, often they come upon the reader unexpectedly. Some of the finest moments in his art are the humorous ones. He deliberately keeps his humour on the knife edge between tears and laughter, between tragedy and comedy. His art (like life) is neither one nor the other, but his humour comes out of that psychic zone where things are both hilarious and terrible, both silly and sad. In *Endgame*, Hamm says:

Let's go from here, the two of us! South! You can make a raft and the currents will carry us away, far away, to other... mammals! (Works, 109)

The term 'mammals' is really unexpected, and silly, yet works to describe Hamm's ever-more desperate psychic state.

Waiting For Godot is full of marvellous lines, most of them hover between desperation and humour. Many of the lines can be performed in a myriad number of ways. Some performances go for laughs, adding all sorts of gestures, faces and contortions to Samuel Beckett's religiously-revered play script (not too difficult for a good actor or comedian to achieve). The opening statement of *Waiting For Godot* veers between comedy and tragedy, ending up usually at absurdity:

nothing to be done. (9)

If an actor such as Max Wall or Charlie Chaplin is struggling with the boot in *Waiting For Godot*, the result can be hilarious, as well as tender and terrible. Samuel Beckett exploits this in-between zone, and in some ways his anti-heroes are classic sad clowns, where the idiotic and cheerful exterior masks a depressed personality (compare with his admiration of Géorges Rouault's clowns).

Samuel Beckett's love of silent comedy, of Charlie Chaplin, Buster Keaton and Laurel and Hardy, is well known. In films such as *The Gold Rush* (1925), Chaplin depicts poverty and starvation in a way wholly in tune with Beckett's middle and late works. Beckett uses many moments of mime which could have come straight out of the cinema of Keaton or

Laurel and Hardy, such as the stage direction in *Waiting For Godot* where Vladimir, Estragon and Pozzo ponder on Lucky: 'All three take off their hats simultaneously, press their hands to their foreheads, concentrate' (WG, 41). The bag/ whip/ coat business, when Pozzo and Lucky first arrive, is an extended pantomime that superbly captures the master/ servant relation, as well as meaning nothing at all (one can imagine Harpo and Chico Marx performing it beautifully).

Samuel Beckett is known as a bleak writer, a teller of desperate stories in which nothing happens, and everything is awful. But Beckett is a great comedy writer, and some of his jokes are sublime. In fact, if there is any transcendence in Beckett's *œuvre*, it is more likely to stem from humour than from night-contemplation or window-watching or desert-walking. Many of the jokes are not jokes at all, but humorous comments on the vicissitudes of life. In *Waiting For Godot*, the verbal gags are as plentiful as the visual ones:

Vladimir: We can't.
Estragon: Why not?
Vladimir: We're waiting for Godot.
Estragon: *(despairingly)* Ah!
•
Estragon: What about hanging ourselves?
Vladimir: Hmm. It'd give us an erection!
Estragon: *(highly excited)* An erection!
•
Estragon: Nothing happens, nobody comes, nobody goes, it's awful!
•
Vladimir: That passed the time.
Estragon: It would have passed in any case.
Vladimir: Yes, but not so rapidly.
Pause.
Estragon: What do we do now?
Vladimir: I don t know.
Estragon: Let's go.
Vladimir: We can't.
Estragon: Why not?
Vladimir: We're waiting for Godot.
Estragon: *(despairingly)* Ah!
•
Vladimir: But you can't go barefoot!
Estragon: Christ did.
Vladimir: Christ! What's Christ got to do with it? You're not going to compare yourself to Christ!

Estragon: All my life I've compared myself to him.
Vladimir: But where he lived it was warm, it was dry!
Estragon: Yes. And they crucified quick.

•

Estragon: We always find something, eh Didi, to give us the impression we exist?

•

Vladimir: Moron!
Estragon: That's the idea, let's abuse each other.
They turn, move apart, turn again and face each other.
Vladimir: Moron!
Estragon: Vermin!
Vladimir: Abortion!
Estragon: Morpion!
Vladimir: Sewer-rat!
Estragon: Curate!
Vladimir: Cretin!
Estragon: *(with finality)*. Crritic!
Vladimir: Oh!
He wilts, vanquished, and turns away.
(WG, 14, 17, 41, 48, 52, 69, 75)

The dialogues have a beautiful symmetry and pace, as if they could not be scripted in any other way. They are endless, the rubbing of old egos together, the scratching of ancient warts and wounds. Two grumpy, old men. Although *Waiting For Godot* has a dramaturgical unity in its action and two acts, the battle of wits between Dido and Gogo could go on for ever.

The two-handed wrangling seems so well-suited to Samuel Beckett's dialectical temperament. Even with one narrator there is still the possibility for arguments between wish/ conscience, ego/ shadow, self/ unconscious, child/ parent, present/ past, etc. The couples that stay together despite constant arguments is not so much a plea for companionship, for emotional bonding, but for perseverance, for keeping going on. Keeping speaking, keeping thinking, keeping striving.

In *Waiting For Godot* the tug is between waiting/ going, between staying/ leaving. But just as important is the battle between speech and non-speech. The prototype pair, Mercier and Camier, debate this eternal Beckettian problem:

If we have nothing to say, said Camier, let us say nothing.

> We have things to say, said Mercier.
> Then why don't we say them? said Camier.
> We can't, said Mercier.
> Then let us be silent, said Camier.
> But we try, said Mercier. (MC, 86)

By the time of dramas such as *Rough For Theatre I* (late 1950s), the double act is tiresome, reaching a point of negation in its unending revolving around the same problems (as in *Footfalls*). The two characters, A and B, bicker *ad nauseam*:

> B: Why don't you let yourself die?
> A: On the whole I have been lucky. The other day I tripped over a sack of nuts.
> B: No!
> A: A little sack, full of nuts, in the middle of the road.
> B: Yes, all right, but why don't you let yourself die?
> A: I have thought of it.
> B: *(Irritated.)* But you don't do it!
> A: I'm not unhappy enough. *(Pause.)* That was always my unhap, unhappy, but not unhappy enough.
> B: But you must be every day a little more so.
> A: *(Violently.)* I am not unhappy enough!
> *(Pause.)*
> B: If you ask me we were made for each other.
>
> (Works, 229)

Of course the characters are made for each other, made by the author for each other to express his particular thoughts on coming and going, on stasis and kinesis, on life and death. It is deeply ironic that a Beckettian character groans that they are not 'unhappy enough' to die. Unhappiness seems to be Samuel Beckett's province (at odds with the general goal of the West, which is towards happiness, towards utopia).

In *Watt* (1945/ 53) a number of laughs are enunciated. There is the bitter/ ethical laugh, the hollow/ intellectual laugh, and thirdly the mirthless/ dianoetic laugh, which is clearly Beckett's favourite:

> the mirthless laugh is the dianoetic laugh, down the snout – haw! – so. It is the laugh of laughs, the *risus purus*, the laugh laughing at the laugh, the beholding, the saluting, of the highest joke, in a word the laugh that laughs – silence please – at that which is unhappy. (W, 47)

The unhappy is absurd because it is the normal way of things. In Samuel Beckett's philosophy, life = pain = absurdity. Humour becomes not a way of letting off steam but of exploring the conflicts inherent in any situation. Humour is essential because it engages life at the deepest level. Nothing can get closer to problems than humour, argues Beckett, and goes on to prove it in piece after piece. In the novella *The End* (1946), for instance, he voices a common worry: thinking you're on the wrong planet:

> You become unsociable, it's inevitable. It's enough, to make you wonder sometimes if you are on the right planet. (E, 91)

This feeling can be stimulated by all sorts of things: the front page of any newspaper; television; fashion; poverty, etc. You only have to consume some of the trivia and banality on television to wonder if you're on the right planet. Surely this Western culture that avidly consumes the gameshow, the reality TV show or the mindless soap opera cannot be yours? Or soccer? Or cars? Or the internet?

The Trilogy features Samuel Beckett's most savage humour, and is freighted with many memorable lines, including:

> Is it true love, in the rectum?... He mused. Christ never laughed either, he said, so far as we know. He looked at me. Can you wonder? I said. There it is, he said... Is one to approve of the Italian cobbler Lovat who, having cut off his testicles, crucified himself?... What was God doing with himself before the creation?... Come on, we'll soon be dead, let's make the most of it. (T, 53, 93, 154, 207)

Samuel Beckett might be right about Christ never laughing. Christianity can seem such a gloomy religion. As Robert Graves put it, there's not one smile in the *Bible* from *Genesis* to *Apocalypse*

In the later works, the clever-clever, pseudo-satircal style of the early works ('the crone smiled from the teeth outward' from *More Pricks Than Kicks* [71]), is dropped in favour of simplicity and immediacy. Samuel Beckett doesn't beat around the bush with his humour. Thus:

> How difficult it is to speak of the moon and not lose one's head, the witless moon. It must be her arse she shows us always. (Molloy, T, 38)

This is typical of Samuel Beckett's humour: to put *moon* and *arse* in the same sentence: for the moon is one of the prime poetic symbols and images, a feature of countless poems.

Much of Samuel Beckett's humour (and portrayal of sexuality) is anal, like James Joyce's (and, curiously, Walt Disney's). Both Joyce and Beckett exalt the anal in things: Pim stabs his rival in the buttocks with a can-opener; Molloy ponders sodomy; the derelict in *The End* farts and defecates in his boat without moving; even words are treated as fæcal matter:

> That's right, wordshit, bury me, avalanche, and let there be no more talk of any creature, nor of a world to leave, nor of a world to reach, in order to have done, with worlds, with creatures, with words, with misery, misery. (*Texts For Nothing, IX*, in Prose, 100-1)

The torrent of words is likened to verbal diarrhoea. As in the writing of Georges Bataille, making art is compared to defecation. Samuel Beckett works in a tradition of anal metaphysics found in the works of the Marquis de Sade, Charles Baudelaire, Géorges Bataille, D.H. Lawrence, John Cowper Powys, Eric Gill and James Joyce (French *avant garde*, modernist literature seems especially partial to evoking anal sex as a cool, trendy taboo). In *Ulysses* we read:

> when he made me spend the 2nd time tickling me behind with his finger I was coming for about 5 minutes with my legs round him I had to hug him after O Lord I wanted to shout out all sorts of things fuck or shit or anything at all... I know every turn in him I'll tighten my bottom well and let out a few smutty words smellrump or lick my shit (675, 702)

It's typical to find in James Joyce's art a childish delight in saying the dreaded four-letter words which still trangress the thresholds of social norms. There is a similar delight in *Lady Chatterley's Lover* and *Tropic of Cancer*. It seems boring and dated now.

Samuel Beckett uses 'fuck', 'cunt' and 'shit' as expletives, driven by anger and frustration. In *How It Is* we find phrases such as 'DO YOU LOVE ME CUNT' (105), and this sequence of internecine fighting: 'when stabbed in the arse instead of crying he sings his song what a cunt Pim damn it all' (74).

James Joyce explained his use of sexual terms in a letter of August 16, 1921:

> It begins and ends with the female word yes... Its four cardinal points being the female breasts, arse, womb and cunt, expressed by the words *because, bottom, woman, yes*. Though probably more obscene than any preceding episode it seems to me to be perfectly sane full amoral fertilisable untrustworthy engaging shrewd limited prudent indifferent *Weib*. (In M. Hodgart, 126)

In the art of Samuel Beckett the wordgames are of a different order. *Ulysses, Lady Chatterley's Lover, The Story of the Eye* and *Tropic of Cancer* and other works had helped to dissolve objections to the four-letter words (or their publishers did). Whereas Joyce had been (understandably) conscious about obscenity, Beckett chooses those words out of necessity.

This is not where his chauvinism is at its most unwelcome. It is in his treatment of women in his art that Samuel Beckett reveals his sexism, which is compounded, as in D.H. Lawrence's fiction and most male authors, of fear and desire. Beckett's work is an easy target for feminist criticism (and has been). If you take the critical approach of second wave feminism (1960s/ 70s), Beckett's texts are tough to defend in relation to the depiction of female characters.

The instances of Samuel Beckett treating women in a negative, patronizing or superficial way in his texts are many. Belacqua handles women sardonically (in *Dream of Fair To Middling Women*, 1932).

Murphy is much blunter than Belacqua:

> Women are all the same bloody same, you can't love, you can't stay the course, the only feeling you can stand is being felt, you can't love for five minutes without wanting it abolished in brats and house bloody wifery. (M, 25)

This is horseshit. Naturally Celia replies, 'I have heard bilge'. But this is by no means an isolated example of masculinist misunderstanding and projection of fear in Samuel Beckett's work. In *Mercier and Camier* some problems arise when Mercier inadvertently uses the word 'yes':

> I said yes? said Mercier. I? Impossible. The last time I abused that term was at my wedding. To Toffana. The mother of my children. Mine own. Inalienable. Toffana. You never met her. She lives on. A tundish. Like fucking a quag. (MC, 84)

Excremental writing in more ways than one. No wonder Samuel Beckett withheld the book for so long. If the men in Beckett's mythology seem ugly and squalid, the women are often depicted as worse. They are dismissed abruptly, or obsessively sexualized. The female body in *All Strange Away* is described with a relish that is neurotic and pornographic:

> say all of Emma. First face alone, lovely beyond words, leave it at that, then deasil breasts alone, then thighs and cunt alone, then arse and hole alone, all lovely beyond words... Imagine him kissing, caressing, licking, sucking, fucking and buggering all this stuff, no sound. (Prose, 119)

It's meant to be dry, distanced, ironic, but Samuel Beckett's fictional treatment of women is more objectionable (and childish) than that of Henry Miller, Georges Bataille or D.H. Lawrence at times (well, maybe not Bataille). Women in Beckett's fiction are either usually old mothers, long-suffering wives or prostitutes. In *Murphy, First Love, Molloy* and others, women are objectified as whores. Beckett piles on stereotype after stereotype. The loathing is impossible to disguise. In *Eh Joe* (1965), the voice taunts him: 'that slut that comes on Saturday, you pay her, don't you?... Penny a hoist tuppence as long as you like.' (Works, 363)

In *First Love* and *Molloy*, sexual encounters with hookers are described in detail. The hobo in *First Love* (1945) is asleep on a bench when a woman starts to disturb him, sitting next to him; 'she began stroking my ankles. I considered kicking her in the cunt.' (E, 15) This is a typical reaction of a Beckettian male. They are unable to deal with people, but when it comes to women their responses can be violently negative.

In *Molloy*, the encounter is more brutal, despite the comedy, despite the tiny amount of tenderness that Samuel Beckett buries under his flood of words:

> Perhaps the name was Edith. She had a hole between her legs, oh not the bunghole I had always imagined, but a slit, and in this I put, or rather she put, my so-called virile member, not without difficulty, and I toiled and moiled until I discharged or gave up trying or was begged by her to stop. A mug's game in my opinion and tiring on top of that, in the long run... Perhaps after all she put me in her rectum... But is it true love, in the rectum? That's what bothers me sometimes. (T, 53)

It is the sort of sexuality you'd expect in a book about a derelict: ugly, brutal, selfish, unemotional, humourless. Of course they meet in a trash heap. Where else? Samuel Beckett is trying to be matter-of-fact, a little tongue-in-cheek, a little humorous and tender, but he fails in every way, as James Joyce and D.H. Lawrence sometimes did when they wrote about sex. It's the portrayal of the sex act that's dodgy, Beckett's narrator's description of it, his attitude, his view of humanity. He's far better when he's writing about itching, pissing, shitting and farting, all those activities that involve one person. When he includes women, the result can be hideous. When the narrator of *The End* quips, 'Real scratching is superior to masturbation, in my opinion' (E, 87), it is fine, and works well.

In the early and middle period works of S.B., women are generally treated badly, both by the author/ narrator and his characters. His is a male world until pieces such as *Happy Days*, *Footfalls* and *Rockaby*, but even Winnie (in *Happy Days*) is stereotyped: there is that laborious spectacle of the handbag and its contents. If Beckett is making ironic comments about women and their social identities here, he is going about it in the wrong way. He is more successful in Winnie's monologue, the way she witters on to herself in that banal fashion:

> I am not merely talking to myself, that is in the wilderness, a thing I could not bear to do – for any length of time. (Works, 145)

If sex appears in Samuel Beckett's art, it is generally men lusting after women or remembering experiences with women (as in *Krapp's Last*

Tape). The gender of the narrator of *Enough* is vague: but the relation is one of sexual power-gaming: 'When he told me to lick his penis I hastened to do so' (Prose, 139).

Many of the texts of the 1960s and 1970s are sexless/ genderless. The visual imagery, the circumscription of complex architectonics, the post-Romantic lyricism, the postmodern allusions and narrative compression take over. The human being as a sexual being recedes, and the body is foregrounded. Bits of the body are noted, as if being dissected on a surgeon's operating table ('arse', 'elbow', 'thigh', 'cunt', 'eye'). The outward inhumanity masks an abstract tenderness and pathos.

Overall in Samuel Beckett's later work there is a movement towards distancing the narrator from direct involvement with humanity in the present. Memory assumes primacy. The texts become valedictory and even, God forbid in Beckett's art, melancholy: in *Company, Ill Seen Ill Said* and *Worstward Ho*, among others.

In *Footfalls, Ill Seen Ill Said, Not I* and *Rockaby*, Samuel Beckett explores in greater detail than before female experiences, feminine power and matriarchy. *Footfalls* and *Rockaby* are particularly powerful, especially when performed by the enormously talented Billie Whitelaw, one of Beckett's favourite actors. Both plays feature women looking at other women, and women scrutinizing themselves in the mirror of memory, in the mirror of the audience, in the maze of mirrors in the mind. (When I saw Whitelaw in *Footfalls* and *Rockaby*, I didn't breathe for the entire, electrifying performance).

The situation of the woman rocking in the chair automatically conjures up classic images of wise, old grandmothers, of generations past, of matriarchal systems, of the push-and-pull of life, the baby rocking in the mother's arms and in the cradle, the beats of the heart, of music, the rocking motion of sex, of people when they are distressed, of comfort, of stasis and motion.

Add to this the taped voice, the hoarse cry for 'More', and those mesmerizing fades of the lights, and you have a haunting presentation of age/ mortality/ memory/ experience/ madness/ elegy:

> time she went right down
> was her own other
> own other living soul
> so in the end
> close of a long day
> went down
> let down the blind and down
> right down
> into the old rocker
> and rocked
> rocked
> saying to herself
> no
> done with that
> the rocker
> those arms at last
> saying to the rocker
> rock her off
> stop her eyes
> fuck life
> stop her eyes
> rock her off
> rock her off
> (Works, 441-2)

Here is an experience of a woman that sounds authentic, and is not patronizing, as in Samuel Beckett's earlier pieces. But the experience is also universal, and with one or two minor changes, could apply to both sexes (or no sexes — much of Beckett's art is genderless, or double-sexed, like Tiresias — the voice of the *Rockaby* extract above could be that of Tiresias).

Perhaps Samuel Beckett's narrators' fear of women stems from the age-old inability of matching the *anima*, the dream-woman, the Beatrice-figure, with reality, with real women. The world defrauds him of a Beatrice Portinari, but instead of exalting her in poetry, as Dante Alighieri had done (which is too euphoric for Beckett!), he goes the other way, and degrades women. Perhaps the fear of exalting Western, romantic love is also artistic: the hatred of over-statement, of Wordsworthian/ Romantic lyricism. Yet Beckett clearly liked that strain of Western poetry and culture, of which Dante is one of the supreme examples (he often cites Dante as an influence).

Samuel Beckett translated a modern exponent of love-poetry, Paul

Éluard (1895-1952). Éluard manages to keep his eroticism authentic and ironic. Beckett translated Éluard's poem 'A peine defiguree' thus:

> Love of the bodies that are lovable
> Mightiness of love that lovable
> Starts up as a bodiless beast
> Head of hope defeated
> Sadness countenance of beauty.
> (Poems, 102-3)

Samuel Beckett rarely wrote in this romantic mode, yet there is that aspect to his artistic temperament, as the friendship between Vladimir and Estragon in *Godot* shows. One can see, though, how any expression of love-sentiments would repulse the austere Beckett-the-artist. Yet there are one or two moments of passion in Beckett's work, and they are to be found in the early poetry. In 'Cascando', the poet allows emotion to overwhelm despair and restraint:

> terrified again
> of not loving
> of loving and not you
> of being loved and not by you
> (Poems, 30)

The lyric could easily have been written by one of the mediæval troubadours (in a slightly different form; although Samuel Beckett did experiment with mediæval forms: *sestinas, albas*, etc).

The terror of 'Cascando' and the brutality of some of *Echo's Bones* (1935) becomes hatred later on. Rejection turns into projection. In their lamentation-like qualities, their obsessive going-over of the past, Samuel Beckett's poems resemble those of Thomas Hardy. The lyric 'Je voudrais que mon amour meure' is particularly Hardyan (Poems, 62-63):

> je voudrais que mon amour meure
> qu'il pleuve sur le cimetière
> et les ruelles ou je vais
> pleurant celle qui crut m'aimer
>
> (I would like my love to die
> and the rain to be raining on the graveyard

> and on me walking the streets
> mourning her who thought she loved me)

In Samuel Beckett's output, love is often of the typical Western/Romantic kind, but grotesquely exaggerated. His view of love is fashionably ironic, world-weary, disaffected, and masculine. It is also of its time: the 1930s, especially. In the 1930s writings of Henry Miller and Lawrence Durrell much is made of womb imagery; poetic links are made between wombs, death, decay, sex and urban life. Womb symbolism (heavily influenced by Freudian, Rankian and Jungian psychoanalysis), also echoes the creative endeavour, in which the artist weaves a womb around herself or himself.

In October, 1935, Samuel Beckett attended a lecture by Carl Jung in which the psychologist, an inspirer of many artists of the time (and still today), spoke of a young girl who 'had never been born entirely' (*Analytical Psychology*, 107).

In Samuel Beckett's art, as in Thomas Hardy's, the belief of never having really been born, or wishing to have never been born at all, is very strong. In Beckett's *œuvre* it is an obsession, and complete obliteration, in a kind of cosmic suicide, is an ever-present desire, right up until the last works, such as *Worstward Ho,* where the text veers from 'nohow on' to 'dim void' (ending it all, you might say, by never having really begun it).

SHOT TWO

PHILOSOPHY

For Samuel Beckett, language and philosophy are bound up so closely together they are inseparable. The linguistic revolution is also a philosophical one. Only language makes epistemological explorations clear. In Beckett's art, a discussion of philosophy is a discussion of language. It is the problem the Austrian philosopher Ludwig Wittgenstein investigated in his *Tractatus Logico-Philosophicus*.

> When the answer cannot be put into words, neither can the question be put into words. (73)

For Ludwig Wittgenstein, the limits of the world (his world) were the limits of language (57). This is true of Samuel Beckett's fictive world. The eternal question in Beckett's work is: is there a world beyond language? Or is language the end of everything? Clearly, in Beckett's art as in most writer's work, language is revered, and hated; it is respected as the means of communication but despised for its limitations, its ambiguities, its inconsistencies, its vulgarities.

Samuel Beckett is incredibly sensitive to language and expression. Full-blown outbursts are an obscenity to him. There must always be some degree of subtlety or ambiguity. He said that 'the slightest eloquence becomes unbearable' (quoted in L. Harvey, 249). Despite this linguistic sensitivity, Beckett is not timid, and happily includes an extraordinary degree of anger and self-loathing in his work, as well as words such as fuck, cunt and other terms. As in the writings of Robert Graves, Vladimir Nabokov and Paul Valéry, Beckett's work looks as if it has been ruthlessly edited and re-written. Like T.S. Eliot, Beckett makes non-stop 'raids on the inarticulate'. The last word in Ludwig Wittgenstein's *Tractatus Logico-Philosophicus* treatise is: 'What we cannot speak about we must pass over in silence' (74). But Beckett does not pass over in silence: he speaks, and continues to speak. Silence may be beautiful, but more beautiful still is to make a stain on the silence.

While he speaks continually of speaking, of language, of expression, Samuel Beckett rarely discusses philosophy. But Beckett's general life-philosophy is clear, it comes thru very strongly, and can be picked up easily from any of his fictions. He constantly comments upon existence, upon what it is to be human. Often he moans and whinges: nothing is good enough. At other times he is wistful, lyrical, or even – God forbid in a Beckettian anti-hero – emotional. In this celebrated section of *En Attendant Godot*, Beckett weaves in notions of mortality, time, silence, expression, ambiguity and mystery:

> Estragon: In the meantime let us try and converse calmly, since we are incapable of keeping silent.
> Vladimir: You're right, we're inexhaustible.
> Estragon: It's so we won't think.
> Vladimir: We have that excuse.
> Estragon: It's so we won't hear.
> Vladimir: We have our reasons.
> Estragon: All the dead voices.
> Vladimir: They make a noise like wings.
> Estragon: Like leaves.
> Vladimir: Like sand.
> Estragon: Like leaves.
> *Silence.*
> Vladimir: They all speak together.
> Estragon: Each one to itself.
> *Silence.*
> Vladimir: Rather they whisper.
> Estragon: They rustle.
> Vladimir: They murmur.
> Estragon: They rustle.
> *Silence.*
> Vladimir: What do they say?

>   Estragon: They talk about their lives.
>   Vladimir: To have lived is not enough for them.
>   Estragon: They have to talk about it.
>   Vladimir: To be dead is not enough for them.
>   Estragon: It is not sufficient.
>   *Silence.*
>   Vladimir: They make a noise like feathers.
>   Estragon: Like leaves.
>   Vladimir: Like ashes.
>   Estragon: Like leaves.
>   *Long silence.*
>   Vladimir: *(in anguish).* Say anything at all!
>   Estragon: What do we do now?
>   Vladimir: Wait for Godot.
>   Estragon: Ah!
>   *Silence.*
>   (WG, 62-63)

Samuel Beckett's own voice is one of those that cannot stop talking about itself, about its life. Winnie, Mouth, Molloy, the Unnamable – these are the self-obsessed, self-expressive voices that never stop talking. The voice is surrounded by void ('there's no lack of void', groans Gogo [ib, 66]), but it is well-equipped to fill the void with its voice. In Beckett's work, when the choice is between void and voice, he invariably plumps for the latter. Speech wins out over silence; but both operate in solitude. Beckett explains in *Proust* (quoted above):

> For the artist, who does not deal in surfaces, the rejection of friendship is not only reasonable, but a necessity. Because the only possible spiritual development is in the sense of depth. The artistic tendency is not expansive, but a contraction. And art is the apotheosis of solitude. There is no communication because there are no vehicles of communication. (64)

This is early Samuel Beckett æsthetics (1931), but the paradoxical doctrines hold good for all of his work. For him, a word such as 'communication' is a contradiction, because there is no communication. Typical too is the emphasis on depth: the implication is that the territory of art has been mapped out in terms of breadth and width, and that the last dimension to explore is depth. One is reminded of (Jungian) depth psychology, and the Zen Buddhist practice of 'vertical meditation'. Beckett himself spoke of 'sinking down' before he started writing.

In a letter of 1937, Samuel Beckett spoke of tearing apart the veil of language in order to get at 'the things (or the Nothingness) behind it' (D, 171). The letter is worth quoting at length, because it discusses lucidly the perennial Beckettian concerns of language, philosophy and silence:

> To bore one hole after another in it [language] until what lurks behind it – be it something or nothing – begins to seep through: I cannot imagine a higher goal for a writer today. Is there any reason why that terrible materiality of the word surface should not be capable of being dissolved, like for example the sound surface of Beethoven's Seventh Symphony, so that through whole pages we can perceive nothing but a path of sounds suspended in giddy heights, linking unfathomable abysses of silence?... it will perhaps become possible to feel a whisper of that final music or that silence that underlies All. (D, 172)

Samuel Beckett here is calling for a 'literature of the unword' (ib., 173), a rebellious kind of linguistic dissonance which usurps the primacy of the word. How postmodern Beckett is here, with his talk of word surfaces, and yet how Romantic and apocalyptic he is when he talks of trying to smash the surfaces of words, to get at the 'unfathomable abysses of silences'. His concern, even at this stage (late Thirties), way before *The Unnamable* and *Ping* and *Worstward Ho*, is with the mechanisms of language. This 'literature of the unword' has its origins in the revolution of the poetics of Arthur Rimbaud and Stéphane Mallarmé.

Samuel Beckett takes Arthur Rimbaud's 'alchemy of the word' and strips it down still further. He extracts the Rimbaudian colour-vowels of synæsthesia and re-shoots the webs of language in black-and-white. Like Stendhal and Gustave Flaubert, Beckett aimed for a translucency of language. Yet many of his texts are as opaque as one can imagine.

For Samuel Beckett, speaking is a kind of being, a kind of living. Words have their own life, but they also help the speaker/ writer to live. And Beckett lives through words as few other writers do. Similarly, his characters are only truly alive when they are speaking or writing. Molloy enjoys his game with the sixteen stones; but just as important is the *relating* of his game. The game of life is in the speaking of it.

Yet the whole enterprise is in danger of being abandoned. The Beckettian anti-hero keeps coming back to speech after abandoning it, like a murderer haunting the grave of the victim. In his last published piece, *What Is the Word*(1989), Beckett wrote:

> folly seeing all this –
> this –
> what is the word –
> (Story, 132)

The whole business is folly – whether of seeing or speaking. 'I don't know why I told this story. I could just as well have told another', says the narrator of *The Expelled* (1946; E, 47). In *Ill Seen Ill Said*, the narrator wistfully wishes for everything to be 'pure figment', pure imagination. If everything was just imagination, it would be easier to kill it, to transcend it: 'Now simple all then. If only all could be pure figment. Neither be nor been nor by any shift to be' (Ill, 20). The question is not 'to be or not to be', but 'to have never been at all'. This is one of Beckett's prime desires: the dream of un-birth.

Samuel Beckett's fictions teeter on the brink of collapse. With his mathematical games, his jokes and puns, his endless wordplay, his irony and comedy, he constantly threatens to demolish the fictive construct. At the end of each piece of the *Nohow On* trilogy the text is upturned:

> Till finally you hear how words are coming to an end. With every inane word a little nearer to the last. And how the fable too.
>   The fable of one with you in the dark. The fable of one fabling of one with you in the dark. And how better in the end labour lost and silence. And you as you always were. Alone. (*Company*, 88-89)

Here selfs talk to former selfs: the figures of the childhood self, present day ego, super-ego/ author and the narrator written into the text are inextricably bound up together, a palimpsest of masks and personas. The scene, of someone listening to a voice in the dark, is such a good image of the writer talking to some part of her/ his mind.

The ending of *Ill Seen Ill Said* is violent, ironic, allusive, lyrical, and total:

> Farewell to farewell. Then in that perfect dark foreknell darling sound pip for end begun. First last moment. Grant only enough remain to devour all. Moment by glutton moment. Sky earth the whole kit and boodle. Not another crumb of carrion left. Lick chops and basta. No. One moment. One last. Grace to breathe that void. Know happiness. (Ill, 59)

Not content with saying farewell in a banal and pseudo-romantic manner, Samuel Beckett throws in a few words which can only sound ironic in a Beckett text: 'darling', 'pip', 'grace' and that last, bitter phrase, 'Know happiness' (or maybe he really means it: *know happiness*).

But it is not The End. Texts extend themselves in many ways: not least in literary criticism such as this study. The end of *Worstward Ho* contrasts the longed-for void with the speech that goes into it. 'On' means speech; 'void' means silence. Samuel Beckett cannot reconcile these two polarities in his art:

> In dimmest dim. Vasts apart. At bounds of boundless void. Whence no farther. Best worse no farther. Nohow less. Nohow worse. Nohow naught. Nohow on.
> Said nohow on. (WHo, 46-47)

Worstward Ho is Samuel Beckett's most rigorous self-exploration. It is the most self-reflexive of his texts. As it travels along it continuously re-appraises itself. It begins, then questions its beginning. It re-writes itself, and becomes a palimpsest of re-writes. Words are invented ('beyondless', 11). There is a delight in impossible sentences which stretch language to its limits:

> Thenceless there. Thitherless there. Thenceless thitherless there... Worsening words whose unknown... Leastmost in dimmest dim... Longing the so-said mind long lost to longing... Less seen and seeing when with words than when not... Unmoreable unlessable unworseable evermost almost void. (WHo, 12, 29, 33, 36, 39, 42-43)

The same fears are present in *Worstward Ho* that were troubling the narrators of *The Trilogy* – namely, what happens when words stop, when the self/ voice stops speaking? There are no words for what occurs when words have gone. Or as the narrator of *Worstward Ho* says it, in that late Beckettian shorthand: 'No words for what when words gone.' (WHo, 28)

Silence is yearned for, but also feared: for silence is terrifying. The void longed for in Beckett's art is not as severe as the mystical Void of Oriental metaphysics. The Indian *Upanishads* speak of a state which is 'unseen', 'unthinkable' and 'devoid of duality' (in R.C. Zaehner, 154). Samuel Beckett's void is a vague state of darkness and silence. Despite the Beckettian desire for extinction, the endings of each text are ambiguous, positing a symbolic in-between zone, somewhere between being and non-being.

Rather, Samuel Beckett's sense of nothingness is more like the German philosopher Martin Heidegger's nothingness: in *Being and Time*, one of his key tomes, Heidegger wrote that we ought to try to experience in Nothing the immensity of that which gives every being its licence to be. That is, Being itself.

In mysticism, nothingness possesses its own kind of richness (S. Spencer, 227). St John of the Cross wrote: 'to come to the knowledge of all/ desire the knowledge of nothing' (in 'Ascent of Mount Carmel'). Samuel Beckett said he was an adherent of nothingness: the quotations from Arnold Geulincx and Democritus are important for him: 'Ubi nihil valis ibi nihil velis' = 'nothing is more real than nothing' (in L. Harvey, 267). Mystical void is endlessly paradoxical: it is supra-conceptual, beyond language, thought, soul, etc. Rudolf Otto defined it thus in his famous book *The Idea of the Holy*:

> By this 'nothing' is meant not only that of which nothing can be predicated, but that which is absolutely and intrinsically other than and opposite of everything that is and can be thought. But while exaggerating to the point of paradox this *negation* and contrast – the only means open to conceptual thought to apprehend the 'mysterium' – mysticism at the same time retains the *positive quality* of the 'wholly other' as a very living factor in its over-brimming religious emotion. (29f)

In Western mysticism nothingness is blown inside out and becomes richness. Emptiness is 'sufficient and great', said the mystic Jan van Ruysbroeck (167). In the work of Samuel Beckett the void is rarely attained. In *Worstward Ho*, the concept of 'less is more' and the void itself are questioned:

> All save void. No. Void too. Unworsenable void. Never less. Never more...
> Less worse then? Enough. A pox on void. (42)

At times, Samuel Beckett attains a near-void in his spartan use of words, placed on the page like concrete poetry:

> what –
> what is the word –
> seeing all this –
> all this this –
> all this this here –
> (Story, 133)

One is reminded of the clean, clear beauty of Oriental *haiku* poetry (such as this poem by Matsuo Basho):

> Journey's end –
> Still alive,
> This autumn evening.
> (In L. Stryk, 89)

Before the void is attained in mysticism the mystic goes through the Dark Night of the Soul, which is like going 'through hell' (W. Johnston, *The Wounded Stag*, 52). Samuel Beckett's derelicts inhabit not a void but a Purgatory, a Dantean zone somewhere between domesticity and despair. The realm of Purgatory is where the ego is stripped of its selfness; 'the essence of purgation is self-simplification', said the Scottish mystic, Richard of St Victor. The characteristics of the Dark Night of the Soul are loss, doubt, loneliness, abandonment, pain, dread, terror, etc. It is a Mystic Death, until only 'one symbol remains: emptiness, darkness, absence' (W. Johnston, ib., 47). It is a 'cruel destitution', according to St John of the Cross. Lost in the cloud of unknowing, at the end of a sequence of punishing negatives, the mystic feels utterly abandoned. But, as William Johnston writes in *The Inner Eye of Love:* 'if one waits in emptiness one comes to realize that the void is God' (121).

Not for Samuel Beckett. When the void, the absence of everything, turns inside out, and becomes everything, what is left is not God, but the self. At the end of everything, at the end of each Beckett text, is the self, the voice, the expression of speech. This is the end result: not God, but a voice that continues 'nohow on'. Beckett paraphrases René Descartes and writes, 'I speak therefore I am'. Descartes ends up with a thinking entity, bodiless, placeless, but still thinking. Descartes explains in *A Discourse On Method*

> I thence concluded that I was a substance whose whole essence or nature consists only in thinking, and which, that it may exist, has need of no place, nor is dependent on any material thing; so that "I", that is to say, the mind by which I am what I am, is wholly distinct from the body... (28)

Total, unenduring absence is too terrible to contemplate, let alone experience, so the writer imagines a voice in the darkness. This is what happens in *The Unnamable*: the Beckettian self reduced to a voice. Even if the voice tells lies, and all is 'imagination dead imagine' and mere fabling, it is still an existence worth perpetuating. There is always this Beckettian voice, behind everything. So many times Beckett created the simulcrum of nothingness – all those negatives piled up on top of each other – and so many times he destroyed it and introduced another voice, another bit of speech.

'The essence of human being lies in its existence', remarked Martin Heidegger. Samuel Beckett acknowledges this: for non-existence is (literally/ epistemologically) unthinkable,. William James wrote in *The Varieties of Religious Experience*: 'there is always a *plus*, a *thisness*, which feeling alone can answer for.' (436)

There is always 'something more' in Samuel Beckett's worlds and texts, and it is the voice. This is the miracle of Beckett's texts: that, despite the pain and loss and general all-round suffering, there is still a voice, still some kind of being with a voice still capable of expressing itself. This is an extraordinary affirmation. Somehow, the thing goes on, whether at the end of *The Trilogy*, or a late text like *Worstward Ho*. A voice keeps speaking at the end of *Company, How It Is* and *Molloy*. And at the end of *Waiting For Godot*, the two once-friends are still together. They say 'let's go' and stay where they are; but the deeper affirmation is not of stasis but of companionship, against all the odds.

In *Worstward Ho* the affirmation is loaded with ironies and provisos, but it is there even so: 'Nothing else ever. Ever tried. Ever failed. No matter. Try again. Fail again. Fail better.' (WHo, 7) Each of Sam Beckett's works plays out this realist ethic of 'failing better'. One could sort through his works and judge them in these terms, of 'failing better'. Later on the narrator rewrites the ethic: 'How try say? How try fail? No try no fail' (ib., 17).

Samuel Beckett's affirmation of life, or of the ability of artistic expression to make life bearable, occurs in a Godless age. 'The bastard! He doesn't exist!' complains Hamm (Works, 119). The attacks against God and Christianity are fierce, but not as violent as those of, say, Bertrand Russell. Beckett's campaigns are really against life – kicks against the pricks.

Samuel Beckett writes in a modern, European age, as ushered in by Albert Einstein, Sigmund Freud, Friedrich Nietzsche and Karl Marx. History, the ego, absolutes, religion and rationality have broken down. Beckett told the playwright Harold Pinter (rather portentously):

> If you insist on finding form, I'll describe it for you. I was in hospital once. There was a man in another ward, dying of throat cancer. In the silence, I could hear his screams continually. That's the only kind of form my work has. (Quoted in D. Bair, 528)

Works such as *Not I, The Unnamable* and parts of *Happy Days* read like screams of pain. Samuel Beckett tries to locate a primal, subconscious, sub-rational realm, where suffering, memory and desire mix. His texts tend to merge into one, like his protagonists. In a sense, his anti-heroes are the sum of every modern, European literary outsider: Knut Hamsun's Nagel, Albert Camus' Meursault, Jean-Paul Sartre's Rosquentin, André Gide's Lafcadio and J.-K. Huysmans' Des Esseintes. The insistent self-referentiality of Beckett's texts adds to the agony. As in Camus' theatre, there is a constant reference to the play-within-a-play, and the staging of it: this adds to the ontological precariousness.

Samuel Beckett writes in a post-Einsteinian, post-Freudian, post-war, post-modern world. Existence is simply *there*, to be dealt with. But Beckett's celebration of suffering is intended to produce transcendence – the transcendence of art, of speaking, of creating. The object of Christianity is to be good, to lead a good life, to be free of sin, guilt, etc, but this is not enough now. The new goal is transcendence and freedom. 'Freedom and necessity are one and the same,' stated Jean-Paul Sartre in *Criticism of Dialectical Reasoning* (377). Perhaps transcendence is too strong a word to use about Samuel Beckett. But it is the transcendence in and through language that he aims for, time and time again.

St Augustine, Dante Alighieri, Blaise Pascal, René Descartes and Arnold Geulincx may be invoked, but the message is Samuel Beckett's own. Beckett is a realist. He realizes that the consolations are few, and generally reside in human subjectivity: in the perception of nature, in companionship, in memories. But not in an exterior deity, nor in Neoplatonic terms of supreme vagueness, such as 'love' or 'spirit'. Absolutes are dropped in favour of experiential facts, which are constantly changing. Beckett realizes that, in the words of Lawrence Durrell in the novel *Quinx*:

> The universe simply does the next thing; it has no programme, does not predict, knows not where it is going. (38)

Elsewhere, Lawrence Durrell says that the universe is a big hug with no arms; that 'you cannot help hugging yourself once you realise that there is no such thing as a self to hug!' (94); and that 'the only art to be learned was how to cooperate with reality and the inevitable!' (191).

Samuel Beckett would not go so far as to speak of hugging (!), but his philosophy does contain, if it contains anything at all, an emphasis on memory, subjectivity, solitude/ companionship and a realism sliding into bitterness. He acknowledges that there is no one else here but us people; that we are merely random collections of atoms; that everything on Earth will be swallowed in the death of the sun; that all consolations are humanmade.

Even so, in this rigorous reductionism, mystery is still present: it is a mystery to Samuel Beckett that some kind of consciousness resides in the random collection of particles that comprise our bodies. The mystery is exacerbated by the powers of language and expression. For Beckett's self is a linguistic construct, an entity that can only reside in words. He seems to record the stream of human consciousness, but he is inventing it too. The anguish of beginning/ ending, of speaking/ not-speaking and of presence/ absence, is in Beckett's philosophy a language problem. It is only solvable through language. His characters only exist in language (for him, but for us too, they have an existence beyond the word). Life may be meaningless, and words have only a limited meaning, but the act of speaking is a gratification of sorts. It's a life, there's no denying it, the Beckettian anti-hero reluctantly admits.

The problem of the self is central to modern mysticism, and it is discussed at length by mystics and thinkers such as Alan Watts, Aldous Huxley, Teilhard de Chardin, Thomas Merton and Martin Buber. For Watts (in *The Wisdom of Insecurity*), the confusion of existence stems from the Western separation of the self from experience: 'to understand this moment I must not try to be divided from it; I must be aware of it with my whole being' (*Wisdom*, 86).

Georg Gurdjieff and Chogyam Trungpa noted how the ego was easily distracted. The great sin of the West, in spiritual terms, is this clinging onto the ego. Yet in the views of writers such as Lawrence Durrell and Samuel Beckett there is a realization that the self and the universe are one. Scientifically, in terms of particles (or our origins in stardust and formation of stars), this is true. The identification in Beckett's philosophy is between self and void, between speech and the silence, between presence and absence. Thomas Merton wrote in *Seeds of Contemplation* that:

> Contemplation... is the experiential grasp of reality as subjective, not so much "mine"... but "myself" in existential mystery. (7)

These ideas chime with the philosophy of non-duality or liberation, which's increasingly popular in the 21st century. Non-duality concepts are perfectly Beckettian: there is no self to even think or live its life.

The least one can say of Samuel Beckett's protagonists is that they realize themselves. Perhaps not completely fruitfully, but they achieve a degree of Jungian individuation. They remain embedded deeply in earthly matters – they do not soar. They do not become the Hindu Self (Brahma), and only rarely achieve the I-Thou relationship of Martin Buber. Like Carlos Castaneda's Don Juan, they soldier on:

> One must strive without giving up, without a complaint, without flinching, until one sees, only to realize than that nothing matters. (*A Separate Reality*, 94)

The transformations occur via language, and the act of writing/speaking is itself a ritual of affirmation. Sam Beckett does not aim to change the world; he is not a moralist, a teacher, a priest, a culture hero nor a shaman. He is an exponent of failure, solitude, irony and humanism. Yet, as opposites turn inside out, Beckett's negations become affirmations. Mystic illumination is not attained, but Beckett's affirmations seem authentic.

There is a beyond-language space in Samuel Beckett's mythopœia, but due to its nature it is not possible to speak of it. Certainly some kind of companionship occurs there. In *Waiting For Godot*, Estragon moans, 'don't touch me me! Don't question me! Don't speak to me! Stay with me!' (WG, 58) This is the kind of primal scream of emotion Beckett abhors. Yet the two men stay together. Vladimir says, 'I missed you…. and at the same time I was happy. Isn't that a queer thing?' (WG, 59) Gogo's response is to be shocked at the word 'happy'. Indeed, it is the wrong word in Beckett's world, even when freighted with dollops of irony.

Not happiness, but a certain kind of harmony born from the rich, perplexing paradox that there is nothing to write and nothing to write with; that there is 'nothing to express, nothing with which to express, nothing from which to express' (*Three Dialogues* [D, 139]). From nothing comes everything. Or at least a little something. Just a little something to tide the battered soul over the next few days/ months/ years/ eons.

Samuel Beckett paints from a black canvas, a void that is the mind: he creates from nothing, with a means of creation (language) which is already there, which already exists in its entirety. All he has to do, it seems, is to pluck the right words out from the sea of language and re-arrange them into some stunning order. The 'world of words... creates the world of things', wrote Jacques Lacan in *Écrits* (65).

As he creates, like a god, Samuel Beckett touches in a host of details. The effect is like Sergei Eisenstein's cinematic montage: instead of a series of images, one receives an all-in-one impression of some event or idea. Beckett does this by his incessant repetition: like views of the same object seen from different sides (the Cubist, 3-D approach). Often the object is the self, or the process of writing (as in *Worstward Ho* or *The Unnamable*). In the late works of Beckett there is a shift: from an investigation of the self (as in *The Trilogy*) to an exploration of the manufacture of a self. In the end it is artistic activity, mirrored in the mnemonic processes of the mind, that becomes the subject of Beckett's texts. In *Ill Seen Ill Said,* the woman appears and disappears; she whitens and blackens; she moves and is still.

Stirrings Still (1988) develops this presence/ absence dialectic in long, unpunctuated sentences (very reminiscent of Gertrude Stein):

> As when he disappeared only to reappear later at another place. Then disappeared again only to reappear again later at another place again. So again and again disappeared again only to reappear again at another place again. (Story, 115)

'Again' is repeated because this is another story, another set of words, another memory, another self fading from white to black and back again. It doesn't matter which story you tell in the end, as the Expelled notes. 'I'll tell you', says Molloy, then adds: 'No, I'll tell you nothing. Nothing' (T, 124). Similarly, in *Waiting For Godot,* the action occurs on one day, a day like any other. It's the same old story, as Clov says: 'All life long the same questions, the same answers' (Works,

94).

Even so, it is still very difficult to end, to stop. Hamm says: 'And yet I hesitate I hesitate to... to end' (ib., 93). The fear may be of not speaking, therefore of not (in Samuel Beckett's terms) existing. Beckett's philosophy is, 'I speak therefore I am', and the consciousness must keep going on.

So the endings of Samuel Beckett's works are problematical: the voices of *Texts For Nothing*, *The Unnamable* and *Not I* never stop babbling. You have to put a full stop somewhere. But the terror of not speaking/ existing is too great. Beckett's people would rather murder than commit suicide, They get close to suicide, but never quite do it. There are 'no words for what when words gone' (WHo, 28), so the void must be filled with words. Total darkness, total silence and (a) total void is never achieved in Beckett's metaphysics. The pressure of the self and its self-creation is too great.

The metafiction never ends. Like Vincent van Gogh, J.M.W. Turner, Mark Rothko and Ad Reinhardt, who all seemed to keep on painting the same picture, Samuel Beckett writes the same story, again and again. The late trilogy, *Company, Ill Seen Ill Said* and *Worstward Ho*, goes over the same ground as previous fictions: the eulogized childhood, the solitude, the being in the dark, the person on the rural plain, the impossibility of ever beginning properly, or ending satisfactorily.

Life is absurd, and a Gnostic rebellion against the wrongness of God's creation helps, but self-creation through writing is Samuel Beckett's deepest ecstasy. Ultimately, he is merely recreating on paper his many pasts. He knows that writing/ speaking is nothing more than writing/ speaking. But for Beckett, as for André Gide, Stéphane Mallarmé, Paul Valery, Rainer Maria Rilke and Robert Graves, writing is living. Or a type of living. The two are one. For some of the time, at least. Any statement about Beckett must be followed by its opposite, as we have noted. Like Lawrence Durrell, in his poem 'Alexandria', Beckett can say:

As for me I now move

> Through many negatives to what I am.
> (*Collected Poems*, 154)

Samuel Beckett's is an art of endlessly 'going on'. The pilgrimage has no goal, no Grail. There is no end-point worthy of being called an end-point. There is only motion, becoming, process, journey. First there is the forest to traverse, on crutches – the forest of symbols (Charles Baudelaire) and the forest of confusion and loss (in fairy tales). Then the track across the moor, the Thomas Hardyan country road, symbol of the quest. The final zone of being is a house, cave, cube, rotunda, cylinder, boat, swamp or abstract space. The rooms are so like cells in a monastery (such as the San Maroo monastery in Florence, which the Renaissance artist Fra Angelico painted so beautifully: a Beckett protagonist could dwell in those small, white-washed cells quite happily, dreaming into Angelico's post-mediæval visions of Christ's Passion).

At times the negation seems soul-destroying (it is meant to be): 'never a gleam no never a soul no never a voice no I the first yes never stirred' (*How It Is*, 106). And if there is a gleam (gleam = life), it is only there for a short while: 'Islands, waters, azure, verdure, one glimpse and vanished, endlessly, omit' (Prose, 145). Between now and never Beckett's texts teeter; absence when it comes is welcomed; but there is always that tiny breath of life, that tiny squeal of the ego to contend with. Thus the woman in *Ill Seen Ill Said* is glimpsed and then vanishes. And everything flickers towards non-existence:

> Absence supreme good and yet. Illumination then go again and on return no more trace. On earth's face. Of what was never. (Ill, 58)

But 'it' (the 'it all' of *Footfalls*), always comes back again. People might fade away, but the will to be, to survive, to *endure*, never dies, it seems.

In the silence there might be no one to hear you scream, but you can hear yourself scream. And that justifies everything, artistically. Thus the Unnamable speaks:

> there was never anyone, anyone but me, anything but me, talking to me of me, impossible to stop, impossible to go on, but I must go on, I'll go on,

without anyone, without anything, but me, but my voice, that is to say I'll stop, I'll end, it's the end already, short-lived, what is it, a little hole, you go down into it, into silence… (T, 363)

In the thereless beyondless thitherless misseen missaid nohow somissaid worsening lidless leastmost unworsenable unnullable utmost unlessenable undimmed unstillable evermost unmoreable Beckett world, the ultimate message is 'on'.

So go on.

In that shortest of phrases, 'on', is Samuel Beckett's total affirmation. And also his total ambiguity. Yet somehow, nohow, he goes on.

ENDINGS ONE

You might end like that. It's an end anyway. Nohow on. Said nohow on. Said on. Said missaid on. It's an end. Unworsenable unchangeable nevermost almost unlessable end.

In the dim. In the void. Go into the void. Said go into the void Beckett. No pain. No bones. Nothing unknown unknowable forevermost pain. Unpainable nothingmost better less forever void.

Save void dim go silence. Till back again. Till void back again dimmest unlessable void. Better worse so. Better on. Better not. What when words gone void still silence. Say no. Then all go. Dim black. Never come back. Void go.

Thitherless thenceless nevermost so-said missaid nohow void blur shades all gone. Never. Add? Never. Remains of nothing ruins a glimpse nohow on still void go burn still silence. True.

Fail again. Fail better. Better next time. Next life. No, not another. Never that. True.

Best worse. Best worst. Worse less worse. No. Less best. A little more. One more time. No back going no time no days no hands no eyes said no eyes missaid no void but nothing. Gone. Dim. Utmost dimmest nevermost leastmost worsemost dim. Unworsenable dim white grey blur black shades dimmost nevermost almost dim void.

Save void missaid void. Go into the silence Beckett. Better worse. Less best. Worse gone. Just bones. It's an end. Like that. Somehow on.

ENDINGS TWO

On. But gently. Careful. See her one last time at the window. Venus rising. She sits still. See her one last time at the window. Motionless. Rigid face. Stony. On.

First darkly. Across the zone of stones. Could say zone of being but nothing matters. See her shadow on the stone. Careful. No shadow. A faint sky now. Careful. Stars then. No. Just immense blackness. No moon she sits rapt before the sky. Gently gently. On.

There she goes flesh no more across the zone of stones say a furlong. Careful. She steps from the pastures into the circus of the circle of stones. Careful. Heap of stones chalk-white all dust kick up and watch settle to earth. Careful. On. Dust settle to the soil footprint like first moonwalks. Careful. No moon. Venus only. And that gone now. On.

She flickers then is gone. White earth with black sky. Nothing more. No more lessness. Snow gone. Dead it's all over. Alone! Loving it. The silence. On.

Loving it the silence said the silence now it's all over. Gone. Careful. Yes gone. Good. No woman no man no stones now. Black night now. On.

No flicker just stillness. Grace. And say farewell. Farewell. The whole thing. Good to feel the void. Breathe in the silence. Not one moment more. All eaten up. First last moment. Now no h•pp•n•ss. No last moment. Know silence.

Illustrations: portraits of Samuel Beckett, and photographs from productions of Beckett's plays.

Samuel Beckett in 1977

Waiting For Godot, Avignon Festival, 1978

Waiting For Godot, 2016

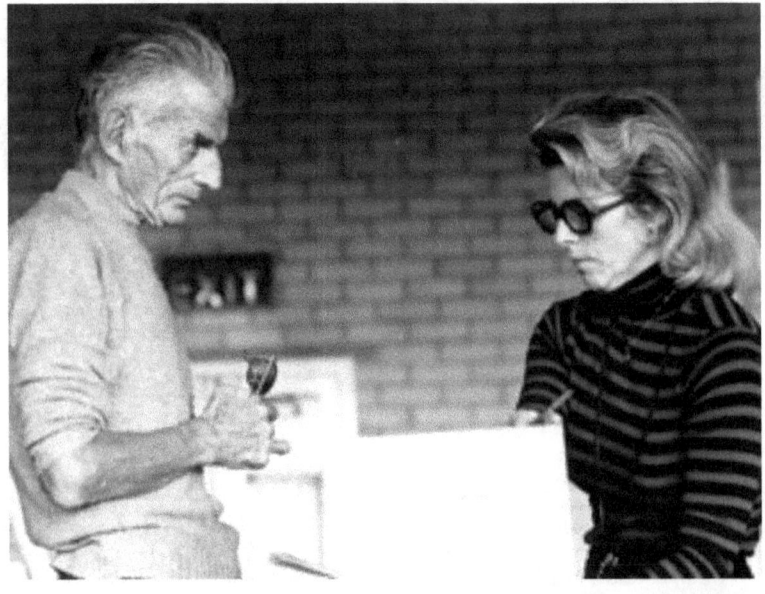

Samuel Beckett and Billie Whitelaw at work

Billie Whitelaw in Happy Days
(© John Haynes)

Billie Whitelaw in Happy Days (1978)
(© BBC)

Beatrice Manley in Rockaby,
Los Angeles, 1982 (photo by R. Goldengay)

QUOTES BY SAMUEL BECKETT

Normally I didn't see a great deal. I didn't hear a great deal either. I didn't pay attention. Strictly speaking I wasn't there. Strictly speaking I believe I've never been anywhere.

•

Nothing else ever. Ever tried. Ever failed. No matter. Try again. Fail again. Fail better.

•

The sun shone, having no alternative, on the nothing new.

•

Then I went back into the house and wrote, It is midnight. The rain is beating on the windows. It was not midnight. It was not raining.

•

Every word is like an unnecessary stain on silence and nothingness.

•

You're on Earth. There's no cure for that.

•

I can't go on, I'll go on.

•

Dance first. Think later. It's the natural order.

•

Don't touch me! Don't question me! Don't speak to me! Stay with me!

•

Let's go.

We can't.
Why not?
We're waiting for Godot.

•

Have you not done tormenting me with your accursed time! It's abominable! When! When! One day, is that not enough for you, one day he went dumb, one day I went blind, one day we'll go deaf, one day we were born, one day we shall die, the same day, the same second, is that not enough for you? They give birth astride of a grave, the light gleams an instant, then it's night once more.

BIBLIOGRAPHY

SAMUEL BECKETT

Whoroscope: Poem on Time, Hours, Paris, 1930
Echo's Bones and Other Precipitates, Europa, Paris, 1935
All That Fall, Faber, London, 1957
From an Abandoned Work, Faber, London, 1958
Krapp's Last Tape and Other Dramatic Pieces, Grove, New York, 1960
Poems In English, Calder, London, 1961
Happy Days, Faber, London, 1962
How It Is, Calder, 1964
Play and Two Short Pieces for Radio, Faber, London, 1964
Waiting For Godot, Faber, 1965
Têtes-Mortes, Editions de Minuit, Paris, 1967
Eh Joe and Other Writings, Faber, London, 1967
More Pricks Than Kicks, Calder & Boyars 1970
Proust and Three Dialogues, Calder & Boyars 1970
Breath and Other Shorts, Faber, London, 1972
Not I, Faber, London, 1973
Murphy, Picador/ Pan, 1973
That Time, Faber, London, 1976
Fizzles, Grove, New York, 1976
Footfalls, Faber, London, 1976
Ends and Odds: Eight New Dramatic Pieces, Grove, New York, 1976
Watt, Calder, 1976
For To End Yet Again, Calder, 1976
Ends and Odds: Plays and Sketches, Faber, London, 1977
Four Novellas, Calder, London, 1977
The Beckett Trilogy: Molloy, Malone Dies, The Unnamable, Picador/ Pan,

1979
All Strange Away, Calder, London, 1979
Compaignie, Editions de Minuit, Paris, 1980
Company, Calder, 1980
The Expelled and Other Novellas, Penguin, 1980
Rockaby and Other Short Pieces, Grove, New York, 1981
Ill Seen Ill Said, Calder, 1982
A Samuel Beckett Reader, ed. J. Calder, Pan, 1983
Happy Days: The Production Notebook of Samuel Beckett, ed. James Knowlton, Faber 1983
Three Plays, Grove, New York, 1984
Collected Shorter Prose, 1945-1980, Calder, 1984
Collected Poems, 1930-1978, Calder, 1984
Worstward Ho, Calder, 1985
Disjecta: Miscellaneous Writings, ed. Ruby Cohn, Calder, 1985
As the Story Was Told, Rampant Lions, Cambridge, 1987
Stirrings Still, Calder, London, 1988
Mercier and Camier, Picador/ Pan, 1988
The Complete Dramatic Works, Faber, 1990
As the Story Was Told, Calder, 1990
Dream of Fair To Middling Women, Black Cat Press, Dublin, 1992
Nohow On, Calder, 1992

OTHERS

James Acheson & Kateryna Arthur, eds. *Beckett's Later Fiction and Drama,* Macmillan, 1987
Robert Martin Adams: *After Joyce*, Oxford University Press, New York 1977
Miriam Allott, ed. *Novelists and the Novel*, Routledge & Kegan Paul, 1963
Deidre Bair: *Samuel Beckett: A Biography*, Cape, 1978
Helen L. Baldwin: *Samuel Beckett's Real Silence*, Pennsylvania State University Press, University Park, 1981
Anne Bancroft: *Twentieth Century Mystics and Sages*, Heinemann, 1976
Roland Barthes: *Image, Music, Text*, tr. Stephen Heath, Fontana, 1977
—. *Mythologies*, Paladin
Georges Bataille: *Literature and Evil*, tr. A. Hamilton, Calder 1975
Gregory Battock: *Minimal Art: A Critical Anthology*, Studio Vista, 1969
Charles Baudelaire: *Flowers of Evil*, ed. M. & J. Matthews, New Directions,

New York, 1958

—. *Intimate Journals*, Picador, 1990

Leo Bersani: *A Future for Astyanax,* Boyars 1978

Jennifer Birkett: *Macmillan Master Guides: Waiting for Godot,* Macmillan, 1987

—. *The Sins of the Fathers: Decadence in France 1870-1914,* Quartet, 1986

Harry Blamires: *The Bloomsday Book: A Guide Through Joyce's Ulysses,* Methuen, 1966

Haskell M. Block & Herman Salinger, eds. *The Creative Vision,* Grove Press, New York 1960

Germaine Bree: *Camus and Sartre: Crisis and Commitment,* Calder & Boyars, 1974

Geoffrey Brereton: *A Short History of French Literature*, Penguin, 1976

William Burroughs: *The Naked Lunch,* Corgi, 1974

Lance St John Butler: *Samuel Beckett and the Meaning of Being,* Macmillan, 1984

John Cage: *Silence*, MIT Press, Cambridge, MA, 1966

John Calder, ed. *As No Other Dare Fail: For Samuel Beckett on his 80th Birthday, by his friends and admirers*, Calder, 1986

Joseph Campbell: *The Power of Myth,* with Bill Moyers, Doubleday, New York, 1988

—. *An Open Life,* Larson Publications, New York, 1988

—. *The Hero's Journey,* ed. Phil Cousineau, Harper & Row, San Francisco, CA, 1990

Albert Camus: *The Happy Death,* Penguin, 1973

Carlos Castaneda: *A Separate Reality,* Bodley Head

Tom Chetwynd: *A Dictionary of Symbols,* Collins, 1982

Herschel B. Chipp, ed. *Theories of Modern Art,* University of California Press, Los Angeles, CA, 1968

J.E. Cirlot: *A Dictionary of Symbols,* tr. J. Sage, Routledge & Kegan Paul, 1981

Jean Cocteau: *The Difficulty of Being*, Peter Owen, 1966

Ruby Cohn, ed. *Samuel Beckett: A Collection of Criticism,* McGraw-Hill, New York, 1975

Steven Connor: *Samuel Beckett: Repetition, Theory and Text*, Basil Blackwell, Oxford, 1988

J.C. Cooper: *An Illustrated Encyclopædia of Traditional Symbols*, Thames & Hudson, 1978

Michael Cox: *Mysticism*, Aquarian Press, 1983

John Cruikshank: *French Literature and Its Background,* 6 vols, Oxford

University Press, 1970
Dante Alighieri: *The Divine Comedy,* tr. Laurence Binyon, Agenda, 1979
Robin J. Davis & Lance St John Butler, eds. *'Make Sense Who May': Essays On Samuel Beckett's Later Works*, Colin Smythe, Gerrards Cross, Bucks., 1988
René Descartes: *A Discourse On Method and Selected Writings*, tr. Veitch, E.P. Dutton, New York, 1951
Colin Duckworth: *Angels of Darkness: Dramatic Effect In Beckett and Ionesco,* Allen & Unwin, 1972
Lawrence Durrell: *Collected Poems 1931-1974,* Faber, 1980
—. *Quinx*, Faber, 1985
—. *The Durrell-Miller Letters 1935-1980,* ed. Ian MacNiven, Faber, 1988
Mircea Eliade. *Myths, Dreams and Mysteries*, Harper & Row, New York, 1975
—. *Pattterns in Comparative Religion*, Sheed & Ward, 1958
—. *Ordeal by Labyrinth*, tr. Coltman, University of Chicago Press, Chicago, IL, 1984
T.S. Eliot: *Collected Plays and Poems*, Faber, 1969
Paul Éluard: *Uninterrupted Poetry: Selected Writings*, New Directions, New York, 1975
Martin Esslin, ed. *Samuel Beckett: A Collection of Critical Essays*, Prentice-Hall, New Jersey, 1965
Julius Evola: *The Metaphysics of Sex*, East- West Publications, 1984
John Ferguson: *An Illustrated Encyclopædia of Mysticism*, Thames & Hudson, 1976
John Fletcher: *The Novels of Samuel Beckett,* Chatto & Windus, 1970
—. & John Spurling: *Beckett: A Study of His Plays*, Methuen, 1972
Michel Foucault: *Politics, Philosophy, Culture: Interviews and Other Writings 1977-1984*, ed. Lawrence D. Kritzman, Routledge, 1990
G.S. Fraser: *The Modern Writer and His World,* Penguin, 1964
Ralph Freedman: *The Lyrical Novel*, Oxford University Press, 1963
Alan Warren Friedman *et al*, eds. *Beckett Translating/ Translating Beckett*, Pennsylvania State University Press, University Park, 1987
Jane Gallop: *Intersections: A Reading of Sade With Bataille, Blanchot and Klossowski,* University of Nebraska Press, Lincoln, 1981
André Gide: *The Counterfeiters*, tr. Dorothy Bussy, Penguin 1966
—. *Marshlands* (*Paludes*) and *Prometheus Misbound*, tr. George D. Painter, Secker & Warburg, 1953
—. *The Immoralist,* tr. Dorothy Bussy, Penguin, 1960
—. *Journals 1889-1949*, ed. & tr. Justin O'Brien, Penguin. 1967
Barbara Reich Gluck: *Beckett and Joyce: Friendship and Fiction*, Bucknell

University Press/ Associated University Press, New Jersey, 1979
Robert Graves: *The White Goddess,* Faber 1961
—. *Conversations with Robert Graves,* University of Mississippi Press, Jackson, 1989
Lawrence Graver & Raymond Pederman, eds. *Samuel Beckett: The Critical Heritage,* Routledge and Kegan Paul, 1979
—. *Samuel Beckett: Waiting for Godot,* Cambridge University Press, 1989
J.C. Greenstein: "Dying Stars", *Scientific American*, 200, no. 1, January, 1953, 46-53
Charles Guignon: *Heidegger and the Problem of Knowledge,* Hackett & Co., New York, 1982
F.C. Happold: *Mysticism,* Penguin, 1970
Clive Hart. *Language and Structure in Beckett's Plays,* Colin Smythe, Gerrards Cross 1986
Thomas Hardy: *Tess of the d'Urbervilles*, Penguin, 1985
—. *Jude the Obscure*, Penguin, 1985
Lawrence Harvey: *Samuel Beckett, Poet and Critic*, Princeton University Press, New Jersey 1970
Ronald Hayman: *Samuel Beckett,* Heinemann 1980
Martin Heidegger: *Being and Time,* tr. Macquarrie & Robinson, SCM 1967
—. *On Being and Time,* Harper & Row, New York, 1972
H. Heine. *The North Sea,* in *Poems and Ballads,* tr. Emma Lazarus, R. Worthington, New York, NY, 1881
Matthew Hodgart: *James Joyce: A Student's Guide*, Routledge & Kegan Paul 1979
Howard E. Hugo: *A Portable Romantic Reader,* Viking Press, New York 1957
Edmund Husserl: *Ideas*, Alien & Unwin 1952
William James: *The Varieties of Religious Experience*, Collins 1977
William Johnston: *The Wounded Stag,* Collins 1985
—. *The Inner Eye of Love: Mysticism and Religion,* Collins 1985
James Joyce: *Ulysses*, Penguin 1969/ 71
—. *Finnegans Wake,* Faber 1964
—. *A Portrait of the Artist as a Young Man,* Penguin 1960
C.G. Jung: *Memories, Dreams, Reflections*, Collins 1967
—. *Analytical Psychology*, Pantheon, New York, 1968
—. *Psychology and Religion*, Routledge & Kegan Paul, 1981
Andrew Kennedy: *Samuel Beckett,* Cambridge University Press 1989
Hugh Kenner: *A Reader's Guide To Samuel Beckett,* Thames & Hudson 1975
—. *Ulysses*, Alien & Unwin 1982

—. *Samuel Beckett; A Critical Study*, Calder 1962
Edith Kern, ed. *Sartre: A Collection of Critical Essays*, Prentice-Hall, New Jersey 1962
James Knowlson & John Pilling: *Frescoes of the Skull; The Later Prose and Drama of Samuel Beckett*, Calder 1979
—. ed. *Samuel Beckett: Krapp's Last Tape,* Brutus Books 1986
—. *Light and Darkness In the Theatre of Samuel Beckett*, Turret Books 1978
Søren Kierkegaard: *The Concepts of Dread,* tr. Lowrie, Princeton University Press, New Jersey 1957
—. *Concluding Unscientific Postscript*, tr. Swenson, Princeton University Press, New Jersey 1944
Ursula King: *Towards a New Mysticism*, Collins 1980
Weston La Barre: *The Ghost Dance*, Allen & Unwin 1972
—. *Muelos*, Columbia University Press, New York 1985
Robert Lapsley & Michael Westlake: *Film Theory: An Introduction*, Manchester University Press 1988
D.H. Lawrence: *Selected Essays*, Penguin 1950
—. *Phoenix,* Heinemann 1956
—. *Phoenix II*, Heinemann 1968
—. *The Rainbow,* Penguin 1981/6
—. *Sons and Lovers*, Penguin 1986
Jacques Lacan. *Écrits: A Selection*, ed. & tr. Alan Sheridan, Tavistock 1977
David Lodge: *Language of Fiction*, Routledge & Kegan Paul 1966
Charles R. Lyons: *Samuel Beckett*, Macmillan 1983
John Macquarrie, ed. *Contemporary Religious Thinkers*, SCM 1968
Stéphane Mallarmé: *The Poems*, Penguin 1977
Andre Marissel: *Samuel Beckett*, Editions Universitaires, Paris 1963
Keith M. May: *Nietzsche and Modern Literature,* Macmillan 1988
Vivian Mercier: *Beckett/ Beckett*, Oxford University Press, New York 1979
Thomas Merton: *Seeds of Contemplation*, Burns & Gates 1962
J.C.J. Metford: *Dictionary of Christian Lore and Legend,* Thames & Hudson 1983
Henry Miller: *Sexus*, Calder & Boyars 1969
Kate Millet: *Sexual Politics*, Doubleday, New York 1970
Fernando Molina: *Existentialism As Philosophy,* Prentice-Hall, New Jersey 1962
Harry T. Moore: *Twentieth-Century French Literature*, Heinemann, 1969
Friedrich Nietzsche: *A Portable Nietzsche*, ed. Kaufmann, Viking Press, New York, 1960

—. *A Nietzsche Reader*, ed. R.J. Hollingdale, Penguin 1977
—. *Beyond Good and Evil,* tr. H. Zimmern, Allen & Unwin 1907/67
Novalis: *Hymns To the Night,* Treacle Press, New York 1978
J.D. O'Hara, ed. *Twentieth Century Interpretations of Molloy, Malone Dies, The Unnamable: A Collection of Critical Essays*, Prentice-Hall, New Jersey 1970
Rudolf Otto: *The Idea of the Holy,* tr. John Harvey, Oxford University Press 1958
Sylvia Paine: *Beckett, Nabokov, Nin: Motives and Modernism,* Kenniket Press, National University Publications, Port Washington, 1981
John Peter: "Our fellow orphan in a lonely world", *Sunday Times,* December 31, 1989, B7
John Pilling: *Samuel Beckett*, Routledge & Kegan Paul 1976
Hema V. Raghavan. *Samuel Beckett: Rebels and Exiles In His Plays*, Lucas, Liverpool 1988
Alec Reid: *All I Can Manage, More Than I Could: An Approach to the Plays of Samuel Beckett*, The Dolmen Press, Dublin 1968
A. Reinhardt. "Art=as=Art", *Art International,* VI, no. 10, December 20, 1960
Christopher Ricks: "Giving death a fair crack of the whip", *Sunday Times,* December 31, 1989
Jeremy Mark Robinson: *Mystic: Love and Mysticism,* Crescent Moon 1987
—. *André Gide: Fiction and Fervour,* Crescent Moon, 2020
—. *Blinded By Her Light: The Love-Poetry of Robert Graves,* Crescent Moon 1991
—. *Glorification: Religious Abstraction In Renaissance and 20th Century Painting*, Crescent Moon 1990
—. *The Passion of D.H. Lawrence*, Crescent Moon 1992
—. *Thomas Hardy and John Cowper Powys: Wessex Revisited,* Crescent Moon, 1991 / 2007
Jan van Ruysbroeck: *The Spiritual Espousals,* tr. Eric Colledge, Faber
Bertrand Russell: *History of Western Philosophy,* Allen & Unwin 1983
Jean-Paul Sartre: *Being and Nothingness,* tr. Hazel Barnes, Methuen 1969
—. *The Psychology of Imagination,* Methuen 1972
—. *Nausea,* tr. L. Alexander, New Directions, New York 1949
—. *Critique de la raison dialectique,* Gallimard, Paris 1960
Arthur Schopenhauer: *Essays and Aphorisms,* tr. R.J. Hollingdale, Penguin 1970
Susan Sontag: *Styles In Radical Will,* Seeker & Warburg, 1969
Sidney Spencer: *Mysticism In World Religion,* Penguin 1963
W.T. Stace: *Mysticism and Philosophy,* Macmillan, 1961

Gertrude Stein: *Bee Time Vine and other pieces, 1913-27*, Yale Edition/ Arno Press/ Books for Libraries Press/ Yale, New York, 1969
—. *Stanzas In Meditation*, Yale University Press, New York 1969
—. *Look at me and here I am: Writings and Lectures, 1911-45*, ed. Patricia Meyerowitz, Peter Owen 1967
Lucien Stryk & Takashi Ikemoto, eds. *The Penguin Book of Zen Poetry*, Penguin 1981
Valerie Topsfield: *The Humour of Samuel Beckett*, Macmillan 1988
Martin Turnell: *The Art of French Fiction,* Hamilton 1959
Evelyn Underhill: *Mysticism*, Dutton, New York 1961
Paul Valéry: *An Anthology,* Routledge 1977
Mary Warnock: *Existentialism*, Oxford University Press 1970
David Watson: *Paradoxical Desire in Samuel Beckett's Fiction*, Macmillan 1991
Alan Watts: *The Wisdom of Insecurity*, Pantheon Books, New York
—. *The Way of Zen*, Penguin 1962/ 80
Ludwig Wittgenstein: *Tractatus Logico-Philosphicus,* tr. D.P. Pears & B.F. McGuiness, Routledge & Kegan Paul, 1974
—. *Philosophical Investigations*, tr. G. Anscombe, Blackwell, Oxford 1968
—. *On Certainty,* eds. G. Anscombe & G. Wright, Blackwell, Oxford 1979
Virginia Woolf: *The Complete Short Fiction*, ed. Susan Dick, Triad/ Grafton 1991
Katherine Worth, ed. *Beckett the Shape Changer: Symposium,* Routledge & Kegan Paul 1975
R.C. Zaehner: *Mysticism, Sacred and Profane,* Clarendon Press, Oxford 1957

In the Dim Void

Samuel Beckett's Late Trilogy: *Company, Ill Seen, Ill Said* and *Worstward Ho*

by Gregory Johns

This book discusses the luminous beauty and dense, rigorous poetry of Samuel Beckett's late works, *Company, Ill Seen, Ill Said* and *Worstward Ho*. Gregory Johns looks back over Beckett's long writing career, charting the development from the *Molloy-Malone Dies-Unnamable* trilogy through the 'fizzles' of the 1960s to the elegiac lyricism of the *Company* series. Johns compares the trilogy with late plays such as *Ghosts, Footfalls* and *Rockaby*.

Bibliography, notes. Illustrated. 120pp
ISBN 9781861712974 Pbk and ISBN 9781861712608 Hbk
9781861713407 E-book

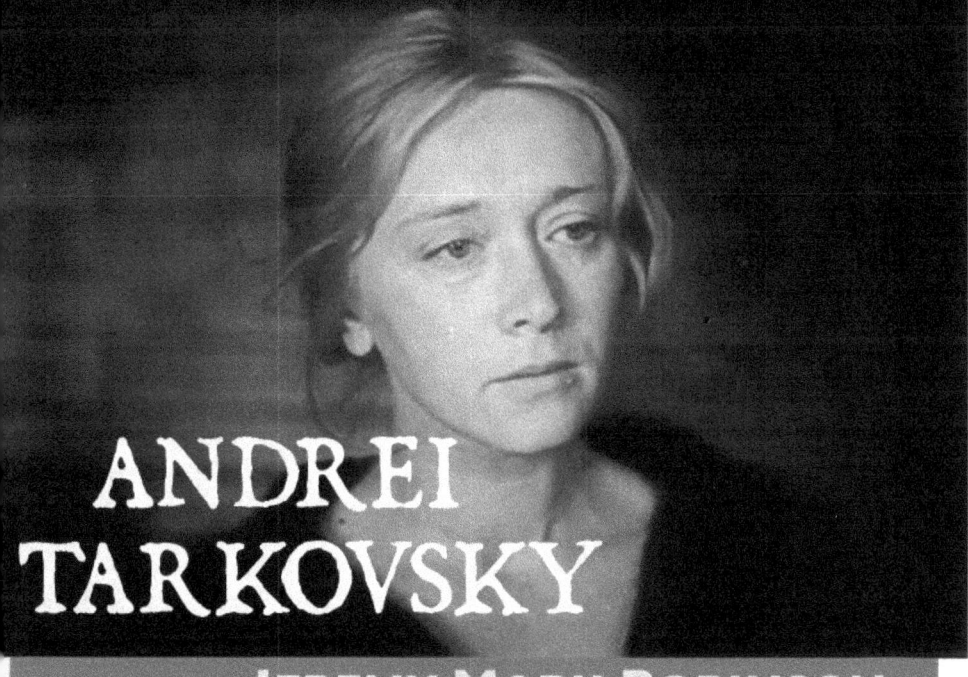

ANDREI TARKOVSKY

JEREMY MARK ROBINSON

POCKET GUIDE

Andrei Tarkovsky is one of the great filmmakers of recent times.

This book covers every aspect of Tarkovsky's artistic career, and all of his output, concentrating on his seven feature films: *Ivan's Childhood*, *Andrei Roublyov*, *Solaris*, *Mirror*, *Stalker*, *Nostalghia* and *The Sacrifice*, made between 1962 and 1986.

Part One of this study focusses on the key elements and themes of Andrei Tarkovsky's art: spirituality; childhood; the film image; poetics; painting and the history of art; the family; eroticism; symbolism; as well as technical areas, such as script, camera, sound, music, editing, budget and production.

Part Two explores Tarkovsky's films in detail, with scene-by-scene analyses (in some cases, shot-by-shot). Tarkovsky emerges as a brilliant, difficult, complex and poetic artist.

Fully illustrated. This new edition has been revised and updated.
ISBN 19781861713957 Pbk   9781861713834 Hbk

Beauties, Beasts, and Enchantment

CLASSIC FRENCH FAIRY TALES

Translated and with an Introduction by Jack Zipes

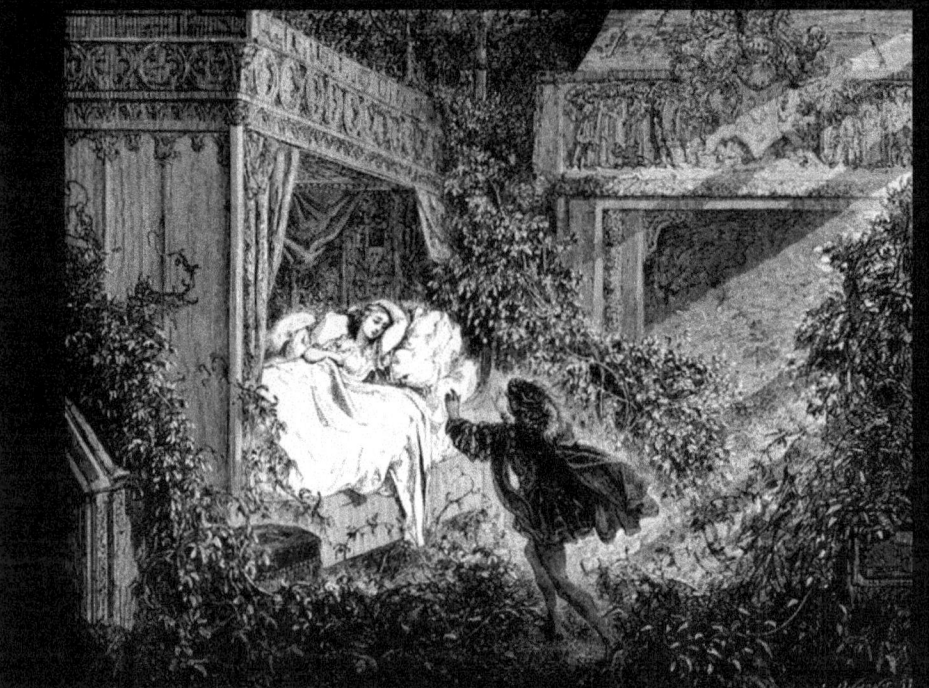

A collection of 36 classic French fairy tales translated by renowned writer Jack Zipes. *Cinderella*, *Beauty and the Beast*, *Sleeping Beauty* and *Little Red Riding Hood* are among the classic fairy tales in this amazing book.
Includes illustrations from fairy tale collections.
Jack Zipes has written and published widely on fairy tales.

'Terrific... a succulent array of 17th and 18th century 'salon' fairy tales'
- *The New York Times Book Review*

'These tales are adventurous, thrilling in a way fairy tales are meant to be... The translation from the French is modern, happily free of archaic and hyperbolic language... a fine and sophisticated collection' - *New York Tribune*

'Enjoyable to read... a unique collection of French regional folklore' - *Library Journal*

'Charming stories accompanied by attractive pen-and-ink drawings' - *Chattanooga Times*

Introduction and illustrations   612pp.   ISBN 9781861712510 Pbk   ISBN 9781861713193 Hbk

CRESCENT MOON PUBLISHING

web: www.crmoon.com e-mail: cresmopub@yahoo.co.uk

ARTS, PAINTING, SCULPTURE

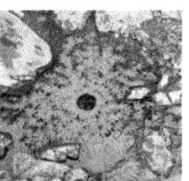
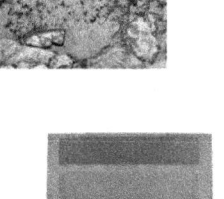

The Art of Andy Goldsworthy
Andy Goldsworthy: Touching Nature
Andy Goldsworthy in Close-Up
Andy Goldsworthy: Pocket Guide
Andy Goldsworthy In America
Land Art: A Complete Guide
The Art of Richard Long
Richard Long: Pocket Guide
Land Art In the UK
Land Art in Close-Up
Land Art In the U.S.A.
Land Art: Pocket Guide
Installation Art in Close-Up
Minimal Art and Artists In the 1960s and After
Colourfield Painting
Land Art DVD, TV documentary
Andy Goldsworthy DVD, TV documentary

The Erotic Object: Sexuality in Sculpture From Prehistory to the Present Day
Sex in Art: Pornography and Pleasure in Painting and Sculpture
Postwar Art
Sacred Gardens: The Garden in Myth, Religion and Art
Glorification: Religious Abstraction in Renaissance and 20th Century Art
Early Netherlandish Painting
Leonardo da Vinci
Piero della Francesca
Giovanni Bellini
Fra Angelico: Art and Religion in the Renaissance
Mark Rothko: The Art of Transcendence
Frank Stella: American Abstract Artist
Jasper Johns
Brice Marden
Alison Wilding: The Embrace of Sculpture
Vincent van Gogh: Visionary Landscapes
Eric Gill: Nuptials of God
Constantin Brancusi: Sculpting the Essence of Things
Max Beckmann
Caravaggio
Gustave Moreau
Egon Schiele: Sex and Death In Purple Stockings
Delizioso Fotografico Fervore: Works In Process 1
Sacro Cuore: Works In Process 2
The Light Eternal: J.M.W. Turner
The Madonna Glorified: Karen Arthurs

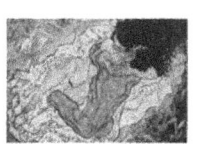

LITERATURE

J.R.R. Tolkien: The Books, The Films, The Whole Cultural Phenomenon
J.R.R. Tolkien: Pocket Guide
Tolkien's Heroic Quest
The *Earthsea* Books of Ursula Le Guin
Beauties, Beasts and Enchantment: Classic French Fairy Tales
German Popular Stories by the Brothers Grimm
Philip Pullman and *His Dark Materials*
Sexing Hardy: Thomas Hardy and Feminism
Thomas Hardy's *Tess of the d'Urbervilles*
Thomas Hardy's *Jude the Obscure*
Thomas Hardy: The Tragic Novels
Love and Tragedy: Thomas Hardy
The Poetry of Landscape in Hardy
Wessex Revisited: Thomas Hardy and John Cowper Powys
Wolfgang Iser: Essays and Interviews
Petrarch, Dante and the Troubadours
Maurice Sendak and the Art of Children's Book Illustration
Andrea Dworkin
Cixous, Irigaray, Kristeva: The *Jouissance* of French Feminism
Julia Kristeva: Art, Love, Melancholy, Philosophy, Semiotics and Psychoanalysis
Hélène Cixous I Love You: The *Jouissance* of Writing
Luce Irigaray: Lips, Kissing, and the Politics of Sexual Difference
Peter Redgrove: Here Comes the Flood
Peter Redgrove: Sex-Magic-Poetry-Cornwall
Lawrence Durrell: Between Love and Death, East and West
Love, Culture & Poetry: Lawrence Durrell
Cavafy: Anatomy of a Soul
German Romantic Poetry: Goethe, Novalis, Heine, Hölderlin
Feminism and Shakespeare
Shakespeare: Love, Poetry & Magic
The Passion of D.H. Lawrence
D.H. Lawrence: Symbolic Landscapes
D.H. Lawrence: Infinite Sensual Violence
Rimbaud: Arthur Rimbaud and the Magic of Poetry
The Ecstasies of John Cowper Powys
Sensualism and Mythology: The Wessex Novels of John Cowper Powys
Amorous Life: John Cowper Powys and the Manifestation of Affectivity (H.W. Fawkner)
Postmodern Powys: New Essays on John Cowper Powys (Joe Boulter)
Rethinking Powys: Critical Essays on John Cowper Powys
Paul Bowles & Bernardo Bertolucci
Rainer Maria Rilke
Joseph Conrad: *Heart of Darkness*
In the Dim Void: Samuel Beckett
Samuel Beckett Goes into the Silence
André Gide: Fiction and Fervour
Jackie Collins and the Blockbuster Novel
Blinded By Her Light: The Love-Poetry of Robert Graves
The Passion of Colours: Travels In Mediterranean Lands
Poetic Forms

POETRY

Ursula Le Guin: Walking In Cornwall
Peter Redgrove: Here Comes The Flood
Peter Redgrove: Sex-Magic-Poetry-Cornwall
Dante: Selections From the Vita Nuova
Petrarch, Dante and the Troubadours
William Shakespeare: Sonnets
William Shakespeare: Complete Poems
Blinded By Her Light: The Love-Poetry of Robert Graves
Emily Dickinson: Selected Poems
Emily Brontë: Poems
Thomas Hardy: Selected Poems
Percy Bysshe Shelley: Poems
John Keats: Selected Poems
Joh n Keats: Poems of 1820
D.H. Lawrence: Selected Poems
Edmund Spenser: Poems
Edmund Spenser: Amoretti
John Donne: Poems
Henry Vaughan: Poems
Sir Thomas Wyatt: Poems
Robert Herrick: Selected Poems
Rilke: Space, Essence and Angels in the Poetry of Rainer Maria Rilke
Rainer Maria Rilke: Selected Poems
Friedrich Hölderlin: Selected Poems
Arseny Tarkovsky: Selected Poems
Arthur Rimbaud: Selected Poems
Arthur Rimbaud: A Season in Hell
Arthur Rimbaud and the Magic of Poetry
Novalis: Hymns To the Night
German Romantic Poetry
Paul Verlaine: Selected Poems
Elizaethan Sonnet Cycles
D.J. Enright: By-Blows
Jeremy Reed: Brigitte's Blue Heart
Jeremy Reed: Claudia Schiffer's Red Shoes
Gorgeous Little Orpheus
Radiance: New Poems
Crescent Moon Book of Nature Poetry
Crescent Moon Book of Love Poetry
Crescent Moon Book of Mystical Poetry
Crescent Moon Book of Elizabethan Love Poetry
Crescent Moon Book of Metaphysical Poetry
Crescent Moon Book of Romantic Poetry
Pagan America: New American Poetry

MEDIA, CINEMA, FEMINISM and CULTURAL STUDIES

J.R.R. Tolkien: The Books, The Films, The Whole Cultural Phenomenon
J.R.R. Tolkien: Pocket Guide
The *Lord of the Rings* Movies: Pocket Guide
The Cinema of Hayao Miyazaki
Hayao Miyazaki: *Princess Mononoke*: Pocket Movie Guide
Hayao Miyazaki: *Spirited Away*: Pocket Movie Guide
Tim Burton : Hallowe'en For Hollywood
Ken Russell
Ken Russell: *Tommy*: Pocket Movie Guide
The Ghost Dance: The Origins of Religion
The Peyote Cult
Cixous, Irigaray, Kristeva: The *Jouissance* of French Feminism
Julia Kristeva: Art, Love, Melancholy, Philosophy, Semiotics and Psychoanalysis
Luce Irigaray: Lips, Kissing, and the Politics of Sexual Difference
Hélène Cixous I Love You: The *Jouissance* of Writing
Andrea Dworkin
'Cosmo Woman': The World of Women's Magazines
Women in Pop Music
HomeGround: The Kate Bush Anthology
Discovering the Goddess (Geoffrey Ashe)
The Poetry of Cinema
The Sacred Cinema of Andrei Tarkovsky
Andrei Tarkovsky: Pocket Guide
Andrei Tarkovsky: *Mirror*: Pocket Movie Guide
Andrei Tarkovsky: *The Sacrifice*: Pocket Movie Guide
Walerian Borowczyk: Cinema of Erotic Dreams
Jean-Luc Godard: The Passion of Cinema
Jean-Luc Godard: *Hail Mary*: Pocket Movie Guide
Jean-Luc Godard: *Contempt*: Pocket Movie Guide
Jean-Luc Godard: *Pierrot le Fou*: Pocket Movie Guide
John Hughes and Eighties Cinema
Ferris Bueller's Day Off: Pocket Movie Guide
Jean-Luc Godard: Pocket Guide
The Cinema of Richard Linklater
Liv Tyler: Star In Ascendance
Blade Runner and the Films of Philip K. Dick
Paul Bowles and Bernardo Bertolucci
Media Hell: Radio, TV and the Press
An Open Letter to the BBC
Detonation Britain: Nuclear War in the UK
Feminism and Shakespeare
Wild Zones: Pornography, Art and Feminism
Sex in Art: Pornography and Pleasure in Painting and Sculpture
Sexing Hardy: Thomas Hardy and Feminism

The Light Eternal is a model monograph, an exemplary job. The subject matter of the book is beautifully organised and dead on beam. (Lawrence Durrell)
It is amazing for me to see my work treated with such passion and respect. (Andrea Dworkin)

CRESCENT MOON PUBLISHING
P.O. Box 1312, Maidstone, Kent, ME14 5XU, Great Britain. www.crmoon.com

cresmopub@yahoo.co.uk   www.crescentmoon.org.uk

www.ingramcontent.com/pod-product-compliance
Lightning Source LLC
Chambersburg PA
CBHW070200100426
42743CB00013B/2990